The Best of
Shakespeare

THE OPIE LIBRARY

The Best of
Shakespeare

E. Nesbit

Introduction by Iona Opie
Afterword by Peter Hunt

Oxford University Press
New York · Oxford

Oxford University Press

Oxford New York
Athens Auckland Bangkok Bogotá Bombay
Buenos Aires Calcutta Cape Town Dar es Salaam Delhi
Florence Hong Kong Istanbul Karachi
Kuala Lumpur Madras Madrid Melbourne
Mexico City Nairobi Paris Singapore
Taipei Tokyo Toronto Warsaw
and associated companies in
Berlin Ibadan

Design: Loraine Machlin

Library of Congress Cataloging-in-Publication Data
Nesbit, E. (Edith), 1858–1924.
The best of Shakespeare / E. Nesbit ; introduction by Iona Opie;
afterword by Peter Hunt.
p. cm. — (Opie library)
ISBN 0-19-511689-5
1. Shakespeare, William, 1564–1616—Adaptations.
[1. Shakespeare, William, 1564–1616—Adaptations.]
I. Shakespeare, William, 1564–1616. II. Title.
III. Series: Iona and Peter Opie library of children's literature.
ᶜᵁᴿᴿ PR2877.N44   1997
823'.912—dc21   97-15223
CIP

3 5 7 9 8 6 4 2

Printed in the United States of America
on acid-free paper

Frontispiece: *Prospero summons a storm in a scene from a 1989–90 production
of* The Tempest *at The Shakespeare Theatre in Washington, D.C.*

Contents

Introduction

Iona Opie

I never think of her as "Edith." It was "E. Nesbit" who took me on innumerable amazing adventures in my childhood and whose books have seen me through the doldrums of adulthood. (It is worth having the flu to be able to go to bed with a large mug of hot tea and a copy of *The Story of the Treasure Seekers*.) And now Oxford University Press has discovered that she wrote a volume of the stories of Shakespeare's plays; I confess I never knew it existed. The book will be a great improvement to my life.

E. Nesbit, who had an original and incisive wit, could also be counted on to be as straightforward as a child, and as refreshingly honest. In works such as *The Story of the Treasure Seekers, The Wouldbegoods,* and *The Railway Children*, all published in England in the early part of the 20th century, she established what is generally agreed to be a new tone of voice for writing for children, one that was not condescending or preachy. Thus she turns out to have been exactly the right person to show what rattling good stories Shakespeare chose to clothe with heartrending beauty and uproarious knockabout comedy.

She says what she thinks, and what the rest of us have scarcely dared to say. We have always thought the Montagus and Capulets in *Romeo and Juliet* were silly not to end their quarrel, that they were inviting tragedy; Nesbit puts it much better—"they made a sort of pet of their

6

quarrel, and would not let it die out." She makes some stringent comments; Lady Macbeth, she says, "seems to have thought that morality and cowardice were the same." This plain speaking is the perfect antidote to the prevailing reverential attitude to Shakespeare's plays, which kills them dead. Such a weight of respect and scholarship lies on them that it can be difficult to shrug it off and enjoy the plays as much as their original audiences at the Globe Theatre in London did. E. Nesbit has rehabilitated the plays as pure entertainment. She tells the stories with clarity and gusto, guiding the reader through the twists and turns of the plot, and giving the flavor of each play by the skillful use of short quotations.

With new enthusiasm, I shall go back to my row of Shakespearean videos, view them afresh as light entertainment at its highest level, and ride straight over the obscure words that once tripped me up. It might even be that I, who was once stuck for the names of any but the leading characters, may be able to comment on individual performances and impress with such remarks as "so-and-so was excellent as Polixenes," but "so-and-so was not at all my idea of Bassanio." Thus E. Nesbit has done me yet one more service; she has given me a belated confidence and enhanced pleasure in probably the greatest playwright who ever lived.

Preface

*I*t was evening. The fire burned brightly in the inn parlor. We had been that day to see Shakespeare's house, and I had told the children all that I could about him and his work. Now they were sitting by the table, poring over a big volume of the Master's plays, lent them by the landlord. And I, with eyes fixed on the fire, was wandering happily in the immortal dreamland peopled by Rosalind and Imogen, Lear and Hamlet. A small sigh roused me.

"I can't understand a word of it," said Iris.

"And you said it was so beautiful," Rosamund added, reproachfully. "What does it all mean?"

"Yes," Iris went on, "you said it was a fairy tale, and we've read three pages, and there's nothing about fairies, not even a dwarf, or a fairy god-mother."

"And what does 'misgraffed' mean?"

"And 'vantage,' and 'austerity,' and 'belike,' and 'edict,' and—"

"Stop, stop," I cried; "I will tell you the story."

In a moment they were nestling beside me, cooing with the pleasure that the promise of a story always brings them.

"But you must be quiet a moment, and let me think."

In truth it was not easy to arrange the story simply. Even with the recollection of Lamb's tales to help me I found it hard to tell the "Midsummer Night's Dream" in words that these little ones could understand. But presently I began the tale, and then the words came fast enough. When the story was ended, Iris drew a long breath.

"It is a lovely story," she said; "but it doesn't look at all like that in the book."

"It is only put differently," I answered. "You will understand when you grow up that the stories are the least part of Shakespeare."

"But it's the stories *we* like," said Rosamund.

"You see he did not write for children."

"No, but you might," cried Iris, flushed with a sudden idea. "Why don't you write the stories for us so that we can understand them, just as you told us that, and then, when we are grown up, we shall understand the plays so much better. Do! do!"

"Ah, do! You will, won't you? *You must!*"

"Oh, well, if I must, I must," I said.

And so they settled it for me, and for them these tales were written.

Romeo and Juliet

Once upon a time there lived in Verona two great families named Montagu and Capulet. They were both rich, and I suppose they were as sensible, in most things, as other rich people. But in one thing they were extremely silly. There was an old, old quarrel between the two families, and instead of making it up like reasonable folks, they made a sort of pet of their quarrel, and would not let it die out. So that a Montagu wouldn't speak to a Capulet if he met one in the street—nor a Capulet to a Montagu—or if they did speak, it was to say rude and unpleasant things, which often ended in a fight. And their relations and servants were just as foolish, so that street fights and duels and things of that kind were always growing out of the Montagu-and-Capulet quarrel.

Now Lord Capulet, the head of that family, gave a party—a grand supper and dance—and he was so hospitable that he said anyone might come to it—*except* (of course) the Montagues. But there was a young Montagu named Romeo, who very much wanted to be there, because Rosaline, the lady he loved, had been asked. This lady had never been at all kind to him, and he had no reason to love her; but the fact was that he

Now Lord Capulet, the head of that family,
gave a party—a grand supper and dance.

wanted to love *somebody,* and as he hadn't seen the right lady, he was
obliged to love the wrong one. So to the Capulets' grand party he
came, with his friends Mercutio and Benvolio.

Old Capulet welcomed him and his two friends very kindly—and
young Romeo moved about among the crowd of courtly folk dressed
in their velvets and satins, the men with jeweled sword hilts and col-
lars, and the ladies with brilliant gems on breast and arms, and stones
of price set in their bright girdles. Romeo was in his best too, and
though he wore a black mask over his eyes and nose, every one could
see by his mouth and his hair, and the way he held his head, that he was
twelve times handsomer than any one else in the room.

Presently amid the dancers he saw a lady so beautiful and so lovable, that from that moment he never again gave one thought to that Rosaline whom he had thought he loved. And he looked at this other fair lady, and she moved in the dance in her white satin and pearls, and all the world seemed vain and worthless to him compared with her. And he was saying this—or something like it—to his friend, when Tybalt, Lady Capulet's nephew, hearing his voice, knew him to be Romeo. Tybalt, being very angry, went at once to his uncle, and told him how a Montagu had come uninvited to the feast; but old Capulet was too fine a gentleman to be discourteous to any man under his own roof, and he bade Tybalt be quiet. But this young man only waited for a chance to quarrel with Romeo.

In the meantime Romeo made his way to the fair lady, and told her in sweet words that he loved her, and kissed her. Just then her mother sent for her, and then Romeo found out that the lady on whom he had set his heart's hopes was Juliet, the daughter of Lord Capulet, his sworn foe. So he went away, sorrowing indeed, but loving her none the less.

Then Juliet said to her nurse:

"Who is that gentleman that would not dance?"

"His name is Romeo, and a Montagu, the only son of your great enemy," answered the nurse.

Then Juliet went to her room, and looked out of her window over the beautiful green-gray garden, where the moon was shining. And Romeo was hidden in that garden among the trees—because he could not bear to go right away without trying to see her again. So she—not knowing him to be there—spoke her secret thought aloud, and told the quiet garden how she loved Romeo.

And Romeo heard and was glad beyond measure; hidden below, he looked up and saw her fair face in the moonlight, framed in the blossoming creepers that grew round her window, and as he looked and listened, he felt as though he had been carried away in a dream, and set down by some magician in that beautiful and enchanted garden.

"Ah—why are you called Romeo?" said Juliet. "Since I love you, what does it matter what you are called?"

"Call me but love, and I'll be new baptized—henceforth I never will be Romeo," he cried, stepping into the full white moonlight from the shade of the cypresses and oleanders that had hidden him. She was frightened at first, but when she saw that it was Romeo himself, and no stranger, she too was glad, and, he standing in the garden below and she leaning from the window, they spoke long together, each trying to find the sweetest words in the world, to make that pleasant talk that lovers use. And the tale of all they said, and the sweet music their voices made together, is all set down in a golden book, where you children may read it for yourselves some day.

And the time passed so quickly, as it does for folk who love each other and are together, that when the time came to part, it seemed as though they had met but that moment—and indeed they hardly knew how to part.

"I will send to you tomorrow," said Juliet.

And so at last, with lingering and longing, they said good-bye.

Juliet went into her room, and a dark curtain hid her bright window. Romeo went away through the still and dewy garden like a man in a dream.

The next morning very early Romeo went to Friar Laurence, a priest, and, telling him all the story, begged him to marry him to Juliet without delay. And this, after some talk, the priest consented to do.

So when Juliet sent her old nurse to Romeo that day to know what he purposed to do, the old woman took back a message that all was well, and all things ready for the marriage of Juliet and Romeo on the next morning.

"Ah—why are you called Romeo?" said Juliet. "Since I love
you, what does it matter what you are called?"

The young lovers were afraid to ask their parents' consent to their marriage, as young people should do, because of this foolish old quarrel between the Capulets and the Montagues.

And Friar Laurence was willing to help the young lovers secretly, because he thought that when they were once married their parents might soon be told, and that the match might put a happy end to the old quarrel.

So the next morning early, Romeo and Juliet were married at Friar Laurence's cell, and parted with tears and kisses. And Romeo promised to come into the garden that evening, and the nurse got ready a rope-ladder to let down from the window, so that Romeo could climb up and talk to his dear wife quietly and alone.

But that very day a dreadful thing happened.

Tybalt, the young man who had been so vexed at Romeo's going to the Capulet's feast, met him and his two friends, Mercutio and Benvolio, in the street, called Romeo a villain, and asked him to fight. Romeo had no wish to fight with Juliet's cousin, but Mercutio drew his sword, and he and Tybalt fought. And Mercutio was killed. When Romeo saw that his friend was dead he forgot everything, except anger at the man who had killed him, and he and Tybalt fought, till Tybalt fell dead. So, on the very day of his wedding, Romeo killed his dear Juliet's cousin, and was sentenced to be banished. Poor Juliet and her young husband met that night indeed; he climbed the rope-ladder among the flowers, and found her window, but their meeting was a sad one, and they parted with bitter tears and hearts heavy, because they could not know when they should meet again.

Now Juliet's father, who, of course, had no idea that she was married, wished her to wed a gentleman named Paris, and was so angry when she refused, that she hurried away to ask Friar Laurence what she should do. He advised her to pretend to consent, and then he said:

"I will give you a draught that will make you seem to be dead for two days, and then when they take you to church it will be to bury you, and not to marry you. They will put you in the vault thinking you are dead, and before you wake up Romeo and I will be there to take care of you. Will you do this, or are you afraid?"

"I will do it; talk not to me of fear!" said Juliet. And she went home and told her father she would marry Paris. If she had spoken out and told her father the truth...well, then this would have been a different story.

Lord Capulet was very much pleased to get his own way, and set about inviting his friends and getting the wedding feast ready. Every one stayed up all night, for there was a great deal to do, and very little time to do it in. Lord Capulet was anxious to get Juliet married, because he saw she was very unhappy. Of course she was really fretting about her husband Romeo, but her father thought she was grieving for the death of her cousin Tybalt, and he thought marriage would give her something else to think about.

Early in the morning the nurse came to call Juliet, and to dress her for her wedding; but she would not wake, and at last the nurse cried out suddenly:

"Alas! alas! help! help! my lady's dead. Oh, well-a-day that ever I was born!"

Lady Capulet came running in, and then Lord Capulet, and Lord Paris, the bridegroom. There lay Juliet cold and white and lifeless, and all their weeping could not wake her. So it was a burying that day instead of a marrying. Meantime Friar Laurence had sent a messenger to Mantua with a letter to Romeo telling him of all these things; and all would have been well, only the messenger was delayed, and could not go.

But ill news travels fast. Romeo's servant, who knew the secret of the marriage but not of Juliet's pretended death, heard of her funeral, and hurried to Mantua to tell Romeo how his young wife was dead and lying in the grave.

"Is it so?" cried Romeo, heart-broken. "Then I will lie by Juliet's side tonight."

And he bought himself a poison, and went straight back to Verona. He hastened to the tomb where Juliet was lying. It was not a grave, but a vault. He broke open the door, and was just going down the stone steps that led to the vault where all the dead Capulets lay, when he heard a voice behind him calling on him to stop.

It was the Count Paris, who was to have married Juliet that very day.

"How dare you come here and disturb the dead bodies of the Capulets, you vile Montagu!" cried Paris.

Poor Romeo, half mad with sorrow, yet tried to answer gently.

"You were told," said Paris, "that if you returned to Verona you must die."

"I must indeed," said Romeo. "I came here for nothing else. Good, gentle youth—leave me—Oh, go—before I do you any harm—I love you better than myself—go—leave me here—"

Then Paris said, "I defy you—and I arrest you as a felon." Then Romeo, in his anger and despair, drew his sword. They fought, and Paris was killed.

As Romeo's sword pierced him, Paris cried,

"Oh, I am slain! If thou be merciful, open the tomb, lay me with Juliet!"

And Romeo said, "In faith I will."

And he carried the dead man into the tomb and laid him by the dear Juliet's side. Then he kneeled by Juliet and spoke to her, and held her in his arms, and kissed her cold lips, believing that she was dead, while all the while she was coming nearer and nearer to the time of her awakening. Then he drank the poison, and died beside his sweetheart and wife.

Now came Friar Laurence when it was too late, and saw all that had happened—and then poor Juliet woke out of her sleep to find her husband and her friend both dead beside her.

Then he . . . held her in his arms, and kissed her cold lips,
believing that she was dead, while all the while she was coming
nearer and nearer to the time of her awakening.

The noise of the fight had brought other folks to the place too and Friar Laurence hearing them ran away, and Juliet was left alone. She saw the cup that had held the poison, and knew how all had happened, and since no poison was left for her, she drew Romeo's dagger and thrust it through her heart—and so, falling with her head on Romeo's breast, she died. And here ends the story of these faithful and most unhappy lovers.

And when the old folks knew from Friar Laurence of all that had befallen, they sorrowed exceedingly, and now, seeing all the mischief their wicked quarrel had wrought, they repented them of it, and over the bodies of their dead children they clasped hands at last, in friendship and forgiveness.

The Merchant of Venice

$\mathcal{A}$ntonio was a rich and prosperous merchant of Venice. His ships were on nearly every sea, and he traded with Portugal, with Mexico, with England, and with India. Although proud of his riches, he was very generous with them, and delighted to use them in relieving the wants of his friends, among whom his relation, Bassanio, held the first place.

Now Bassanio, like many another gay and gallant gentleman, was reckless and extravagant, and finding that he had not only come to the end of his fortune, but was also unable to pay his creditors, he went to Antonio for further help.

"To you, Antonio," he said, "I owe the most in money and in love: and I have thought of a plan to pay everything I owe if you will but help me."

"Say what I can do, and it shall be done," answered his friend.

Then said Bassanio, "In Belmont is a lady richly left, and from all quarters of the globe renowned suitors come to woo her, not only because she is rich, but because she is beautiful and good as well. She looked on me with such favor when last we met, that I feel sure that I should win her away from all rivals for her love had I but the means to go to Belmont, where she lives."

"All my fortunes," said Antonio, "are at sea, and so I have no ready money; but luckily my credit is good in Venice, and I will borrow for you what you need."

There was living in Venice at this time a rich money-lender, named Shylock. Antonio despised and disliked this man very much, and treated him with the greatest harshness and scorn. He would thrust him, like a dog, over his threshold, and would even spit on him. Shylock submitted to all these indignities with a patient shrug; but deep in his heart he cherished a desire for revenge on the rich, smug merchant. For Antonio both hurt his pride and injured his business. "But for him," thought Shylock, "I would be richer by half a million ducats. On the market place, and wherever he can, he denounces the rate of interest I charge, and—worse than that—he lends out money freely."

So when Bassanio came to him to ask for a loan of three thousand ducats to Antonio for three months, Shylock hid his hatred, and turning to Antonio, said—"Harshly as you have treated me, I would be friends with you and have your love. So I will lend you the money and charge you no interest. But, just for fun, you shall sign a bond in which it shall be agreed that if you do not repay me in three months' time, then I shall have the right to a pound of your flesh, to be cut from what part of your body I choose."

"No," cried Bassanio to his friend, "you shall run no such risk for me."

"Why, fear not," said Antonio, "my ships will be home a month before the time. I will sign the bond."

Thus Bassanio was furnished with the means to go to Belmont, there to woo the lovely Portia. The very night he started, the money-lender's pretty daughter, Jessica, ran away from her father's house with her lover, and she took with her from her father's hoards some bags of ducats and precious stones. Shylock's grief and anger were terrible to see. His love for her changed to hate. "I wish she were dead at my feet and the jewels in her ear," he cried. His only comfort now was in hearing of the serious losses which had befallen Antonio, some of whose ships were wrecked. "Let him look to his bond," said Shylock, "let him look to his bond."

Meanwhile Bassanio had reached Belmont, and had visited the fair Portia. He found, as he had told Antonio, that the rumor of her wealth and beauty had drawn to her suitors from far and near. But to all of them Portia had but one reply. She would only accept that suitor who would pledge himself to abide by the terms of her father's will. These were conditions that frightened away many an ardent wooer. For he who would win Portia's heart and hand, had to guess which of three caskets held her portrait. If he guessed aright, then Portia would be his bride; if wrong, then he was bound by oath never to reveal which casket he chose, never to marry, and to go away at once.

The caskets were of gold, silver, and lead. The gold one bore this inscription: "Who chooseth me shall gain what many men desire"; the silver one had this: "Who chooseth me shall get as much as he deserves"; while on the lead one were these words: "Who chooseth me must give and hazard all he hath." The Prince of Morocco, as brave as he was black, was among the first to submit to this test. He chose the gold casket, for he said neither base lead nor silver could contain her picture. So he chose the gold casket, and found inside the likeness of what many men desire—death.

After him came the haughty Prince of Arragon, and saying, "Let me have what I deserve—surely I deserve the lady," he chose the silver one, and found inside a fool's head. "Did I deserve no more than a fool's head?" he cried.

Then at last came Bassanio, and Portia would have delayed him from making his choice from very fear of his choosing wrong. For she loved

"Mere outward show," he said, "is to be despised. The world is
still deceived with ornament, and so no gaudy gold or shining silver
for me. I choose the lead casket; joy be the consequence!"

him dearly, even as he loved her. "But," said Bassanio, "let me choose at once, for, as I am, I live upon the rack."

Then Portia asked her servants to bring music and play while her gallant lover made his choice. And Bassanio took the oath and walked up to the caskets—the musicians playing softly the while. "Mere outward show," he said, "is to be despised. The world is still deceived with ornament, and so no gaudy gold or shining silver for me. I choose the lead casket; joy be the consequence!" And opening it, he found fair Portia's portrait inside, and he turned to her and asked if it were true that she was his.

"Yes," said Portia, "I am yours, and this house is yours, and with them I give you this ring, from which you must never part."

And Bassanio, saying that he could hardly speak for joy, found words to swear that he would never part with the ring while he lived.

Then suddenly all his happiness was dashed with sorrow, for messengers came from Venice to tell him that Antonio was ruined, and that Shylock demanded from the Duke the fulfilment of the bond, under which he was entitled to a pound of the merchant's flesh. Portia was as grieved as Bassanio to hear of the danger which threatened his friend.

· "First," she said, "take me to the church and make me your wife, and then go to Venice at once to help your friend. You shall take with you money enough to pay his debt twenty times over."

Portia arrived in her disguise.... Then in noble words she bade Shylock
have mercy.... "I will have the pound of flesh," was his reply.

But when her newly-made husband had gone, Portia went after him, and arrived in Venice disguised as a lawyer, and with an introduction from a celebrated lawyer named Bellario, whom the Duke of Venice had called in to decide the legal questions raised by Shylock's claim to a pound of Antonio's flesh. When the Court met, Bassanio offered Shylock twice the money borrowed, if he would withdraw his claim. But the money-lender's only answer was:

"If every ducat in six thousand ducat
Were in six parts, and every part a ducat,
I would not draw them—I would have my bond."

It was then that Portia arrived in her disguise, and not even her own husband knew her. The Duke gave her welcome on account of the great Bellario's introduction, and left the settlement of the case to her. Then in noble words she bade Shylock have mercy. But he was deaf to her entreaties. "I will have the pound of flesh," was his reply.

"What have you to say?" asked Portia of the merchant.

"But little," he answered; "I am armed and well prepared."

"The Court awards you a pound of Antonio's flesh," said Portia to the money-lender.

"Most righteous judge!" cried Shylock. "A sentence: come, prepare."

"Wait a little. This bond gives you no right to Antonio's blood, only to his flesh. If, then, you spill a drop of his blood, all your property will be forfeited to the State. Such is the Law."

And Shylock, in his fear, said, "Then I will take Bassanio's offer."

"No," said Portia sternly, "you shall have nothing but your bond. Take your pound of flesh, but remember, that if you take more or less, even by the weight of a hair, you will lose your property and your life."

"No," said Portia sternly, "you shall have nothing but your bond. Take your pound of flesh, but remember, that if you take more or less, even by the weight of a hair, you will lose your property and your life."

Shylock now grew very much frightened. "Give me my three thousand ducats that I lent him, and let him go."

Bassanio would have paid it to him, but said Portia, "No! He shall have nothing but his bond."

"You, a foreigner," she added, "have sought to take the life of a Venetian citizen, and thus by the Venetian law, your life and goods are forfeited. Down, therefore, and beg mercy of the Duke."

Thus were the tables turned, and no mercy would have been shown to Shylock, had it not been for Antonio. As it was, the money-lender forfeited half his fortune to the State, and he had to settle the other half on his daughter's husband, and with this he had to be content.

Bassanio, in his gratitude to the clever lawyer, was induced to part with the ring his wife had given him, and with which he had promised never to part, and when on his return to Belmont he confessed as much to Portia, she seemed very angry, and vowed she would not be friends with him until she had her ring again. But at last she told him that it was she who, in the disguise of a lawyer, had saved his friend's life, and got the ring from him. So Bassanio was forgiven, and made happier than ever, to know how rich a prize he had drawn in the lottery of the caskets.

Twelfth Night

Orsino, the Duke of Illyria, was deeply in love with a beautiful Countess, named Olivia. Yet was all his love in vain, for she disdained his suit; and when her brother died, she sent back a messenger from the Duke, bidding him tell his master that for seven years she would not let the very air behold her face, but that, like a nun, she would walk veiled; and all this for the sake of a dead brother's love, which she would keep fresh and lasting in her sad remembrance.

The Duke longed for someone to whom he could tell his sorrow, and repeat over and over again the story of his love. And chance brought him such a companion. For about this time a goodly ship was wrecked on the Illyrian coast, and among those who reached land in safety were the Captain and a fair young maid, named Viola. But she was little grateful for being rescued from the perils of the sea, since she feared that her twin brother was drowned, Sebastian, as dear to her as the heart in her bosom, and so like her that, but for the difference in their manner of dress, one could hardly be told from the other. The Captain, for her comfort, told her that he had seen her brother bind himself to a

Viola unwittingly went on this errand, but when she came to the house, Malvolio . . . a vain, officious man . . . forbade her entrance.

strong mast that lived upon the sea, and that thus there was hope that he might be saved.

Viola now asked in whose country she was, and learning that the young Duke Orsino ruled there, and was as noble in his nature as in his name, she decided to disguise herself in male attire, and seek for employment with him as a page.

In this she succeeded, and now from day to day she had to listen to the story of Orsino's love. At first she sympathized very truly with him, but soon her sympathy grew to love. At last it occurred to Orsino that his hopeless love-suit might prosper better if he sent this pretty lad to woo Olivia for him. Viola unwillingly went on this errand, but when she came to the house, Malvolio, Olivia's steward, a vain, officious man, sick, as his mistress told him, of self-love, forbade the messenger admittance. Viola, however, (who was now called Cesario) refused to take any denial, and vowed to speak with the Countess. Olivia, hearing how her instructions were defied and curious to see this daring youth, said, "We'll once more hear Orsino's plea."

When Viola was admitted to her presence and the servants had been sent away, she listened patiently to the reproaches which this bold messenger from the Duke poured upon her, and listening, she fell in love with the supposed Cesario; and when Cesario had gone, Olivia longed to send some love-token after him. So, calling Malvolio, she bade him follow the boy.

"He left this ring behind him," she said, taking one from her finger. "Tell him I will none of it."

Malvolio did as he was bid, and then Viola, who of course knew perfectly well that she had left no ring behind her, saw with a woman's quickness that Olivia loved her. Then she went back to the Duke, very sad at heart for her lover, and for Olivia, and for herself.

It was but cold comfort she could give Orsino, who now sought to ease the pangs of despised love by listening to sweet music, while Cesario

◆

She listened patiently to the reproaches which this bold messenger from the Duke poured upon her, and listening, she fell in love with the supposed Cesario.

stood by his side. "Ah," said the Duke to his page that night, "you too have been in love."

"A little," answered Viola.

"What kind of woman is it?" he asked.

"Of your complexion," she answered.

"What years?" was his next question.

To this came the pretty answer, "About your years, my lord."

"Too old, by Heaven!" cried the Duke. "Let still the woman take an elder than herself."

And Viola very meekly said, "I think it well, my lord."

By and by Orsino begged Cesario once more to visit Olivia and to plead his love-suit. But she, thinking to dissuade him, said:

"If some lady loved you as you love Olivia?"

"Ah! that cannot be," said the Duke.

"But I know," Viola went on, "what love woman may have for a man. My father had a daughter loved a man, as it might be," she added blushing, "perhaps, were I a woman, I should love your lordship."

"And what is her history?" he asked.

"A blank, my lord," Viola answered. "She never told her love, but let concealment like a worm in the bud feed on her cheek; she pined in thought, and with a green and yellow melancholy she sat, like Patience on a monument, smiling at grief. Was not this love indeed?"

"But died thy sister of her love, my boy?" the Duke asked; and Viola, who had all the time been telling her own love for him in this pretty fashion, said:

"I am all the daughters my father has and all the brothers—Sir, shall I go to the lady?"

"To her in haste," said the Duke, at once forgetting all about the story, "and give her this jewel."

So Viola went, and this time poor Olivia was unable to hide her love, and openly confessed it with such passionate truth, that Viola left her hastily, saying:

"Nevermore will I deplore my master's tears to you."

But in vowing this, Viola did not know the tender pity she would feel for other's suffering. So when Olivia, in the violence of her love, sent a messenger, asking Cesario to visit her once more, Cesario had no heart to refuse the request.

But the favors which Olivia bestowed upon this mere page aroused the jealousy of Sir Andrew Aguecheek, a foolish, rejected lover of hers, who at that time was staying at her house with her merry old uncle Sir Toby. This same Sir Toby dearly loved a practical joke, and knowing Sir Andrew to be an coward, he thought that if he could bring off a duel between him and Cesario, there would be brave sport indeed. So he induced Sir Andrew to send a challenge, which he himself took to Cesario. The poor page, in great terror, said:

"I will return again to the house, I am no fighter."

"Back you shall not to the house," said Sir Toby, "unless you fight me first."

And as he looked a very fierce old gentleman, Viola thought it best to await Sir Andrew's coming; and when he at last made his appearance, in a great fright, if the truth had been known, she trembling drew her sword, and Sir Andrew in like fear followed her example. Happily for them both, at this moment some officers of the Court came on the scene, and stopped the intended duel. Viola gladly made off with what speed she might, while Sir Toby called after her:

"A very paltry boy, and more a coward than a hare!"

Now, while these things were happening, Sebastian had escaped all the dangers of the deep, and had landed safely in Illyria, where he determined to make his way to the Duke's Court. On his way there he passed Olivia's house just as Viola had left it in such a hurry, and whom should

♦

This same Sir Toby dearly loved a practical joke.

he meet but Sir Andrew and Sir Toby? Sir Andrew, mistaking Sebastian for the cowardly Cesario, took his courage in both hands, and walking up to him struck him, saying, "There's for you."

"Why, there's for you; and there, and there!" said Sebastian, hitting back a great deal harder, and again and again, till Sir Toby came to the rescue of his friend. Sebastian, however, tore himself free from Sir Toby's clutches, and drawing his sword would have fought them both, but that Olivia herself, having heard of the quarrel, came running in, and with many reproaches sent Sir Toby and his friend away. Then turning to Sebastian, whom she too thought to be Cesario, she besought him with many a pretty speech to come into the house with her.

Sebastian, half dazed and all delighted with her beauty and grace, readily consented, and that very day, so great was Olivia's haste, they were married before she had discovered that he was not Cesario, or Sebastian was quite certain whether or not he was in a dream.

Meanwhile Orsino, hearing how Cesario fled with Olivia, visited her himself, taking Cesario with him. Olivia met them before her door, and seeing, as she thought, her husband there, reproached him for leaving her, while to the Duke she said that his suit was as fat and wholesome to her as howling after music.

"Still so cruel?" said Orsino.

"Still so constant," she answered.

Then Orsino's anger growing to cruelty, he vowed that, to be revenged on her, he would kill Cesario, whom he knew she loved. "Come, boy," he said to the page.

And Viola, following him as he moved away, said, "I, to do you rest, a thousand deaths would die."

A great fear took hold on Olivia, and she cried aloud, "Cesario, husband, stay!"

"Her husband?" asked the Duke angrily.

"No, my lord, not I," said Viola.

"Call forth the holy father," cried Olivia.

And the priest who had married Sebastian and Olivia, coming in, declared Cesario to be the bridegroom.

"O thou lying cub!" the Duke exclaimed. "Farewell, and take her, but go where thou and I henceforth may never meet."

At this moment Sir Andrew Aguecheek came up with a bleeding head, complaining that Cesario had broken it, and Sir Toby's as well.

"I never hurt you," said Viola, very positively; "you drew your sword on me, but I bespoke you fair, and hurt you not."

Yet, for all her protesting, no one there believed her; but all their thoughts were on a sudden changed to wonder, when Sebastian came in.

"I am sorry, madam," he said to his wife, "I have hurt your kinsman. Pardon me, sweet, even for the vows we made each other so late ago."

"One face, one voice, one habit, and two persons!" cried the Duke, looking first at Viola, and then at Sebastian.

"An apple cleft in two," said one who knew Sebastian, "is not more twin than these two creatures. Which is Sebastian?"

"I never had a brother," said Sebastian. "I had a sister, whom the blind waves and surges have devoured. Were you a woman," he said to Viola, "I should let my tears fall upon your cheek, and say, 'Thrice welcome, drowned Viola!'"

Then Viola, rejoicing to see her dear brother alive, confessed that she was indeed his sister, Viola. As she spoke, Orsino felt the pity that is akin to love.

"Boy," he said, "thou hast said to me a thousand times thou never shouldst love woman like to me."

"And all those sayings will I over-swear," Viola replied, "and all those swearings keep true."

"Give me thy hand," Orsino cried in gladness. "Thou shalt be my wife, and my fancy's queen."

Thus was the gentle Viola made happy, while Olivia found in Sebastian a constant lover, and a good husband, and he in her a true and loving wife.

Hamlet

*H*amlet was the only son of the King of Denmark. He loved his father and mother dearly—and was happy in the love of a sweet lady named Ophelia. Her father, Polonius, was the King's chancellor.

While Hamlet was away studying at Wittenberg, his father died. Young Hamlet hastened home in great grief to hear that a serpent had stung the King, and that he was dead. The young prince had loved his father tenderly—so you may judge what he felt when he found that the Queen, before yet the King had been laid in the ground a month, had determined to marry again—and to marry the dead King's brother.

Hamlet refused to put off his mourning for the wedding.

"It is not only the black I wear on my body," he said, "that proves my loss. I wear mourning in my heart for my dead father. His son at least remembers him, and grieves still."

Then said Claudius, the King's brother, "This grief is unreasonable. Of course you must sorrow at the loss of your father, but—"

"Ah," said Hamlet, bitterly, "I cannot in one little month forget those I love."

With that the Queen and Claudius left him, to make merry over their wedding, forgetting the poor good King who had been so kind to them both.

And Hamlet, left alone, began to wonder and to question as to what he ought to do. For he could not believe the story about the snake-bite. It seemed to him all too plain that the wicked Claudius had killed the King, so as to get the crown and marry the Queen. Yet he had no proof, and could not accuse Claudius.

And while he was thus thinking came Horatio, a fellow student of his, from Wittenberg.

"What brought you here?" asked Hamlet, when he had greeted his friend kindly.

"I came, my lord, to see your father's funeral."

"I think it was to see my mother's wedding," said Hamlet, bitterly. "My father! We shall not look upon his like again."

"My lord," answered Horatio, "I think I saw him yesternight."

Then, while Hamlet listened in surprise, Horatio told how he, with two gentlemen of the guard, had seen the King's ghost on the battlements. Hamlet went that night, and true enough, at midnight, the ghost of the King, in the armor he used to wear, appeared on the battlements in the chill moonlight. Hamlet was a brave youth. Instead of running away from the ghost he spoke to it—and when it beckoned him he followed it to a quiet place, and there the ghost told him what he had suspected was true. The wicked Claudius had indeed killed his good brother the King, by dropping poison into his ear as he slept in his orchard in the afternoon.

"And you," said the ghost, "must avenge this cruel murder—on my wicked brother. But do nothing against the Queen, for I have loved her, and she is thy mother. Remember me."

Then seeing the morning approach, the ghost vanished.

"Now," said Hamlet, "there is nothing left but revenge. Remember

"And you," said the ghost, "must avenge this cruel murder—on my wicked brother. But do nothing against the Queen, for I have loved her, and she is thy mother."

thee—I will remember nothing else—books, pleasure, youth—let all go—and your commands alone live on my brain."

So when his friends came back he made them swear to keep the secret of the ghost, and then went in from the battlements, now gray with mingled dawn and moonlight, to think how he might best avenge his murdered father.

The shock of seeing and hearing his father's ghost made him feel almost mad, and for fear that his uncle might notice that he was not himself, he determined to hide his mad longing for revenge under a pretended madness in other matters.

And when he met Ophelia, who loved him—and to whom he had given gifts, and letters, and many loving words—he behaved so wildly to her, that she could not but think him mad. For she loved him so that she could not believe he would be so cruel as this, unless he were quite mad. So she told her father, and showed him a pretty letter from Hamlet. And in the letter was much folly, and this pretty verse:

> *"Doubt that the stars are fire;*
> *Doubt that the sun doth move;*
> *Doubt truth to be a liar;*
> *But never doubt I love."*

And from that time everyone believed that the cause of Hamlet's supposed madness was love.

Poor Hamlet was very unhappy. He longed to obey his father's ghost—and yet he was too gentle and kindly to wish to kill another man, even his father's murderer. And sometimes he wondered whether, after all, the ghost spoke truly.

Just at this time some actors came to the Court, and Hamlet ordered them to perform a certain play before the King and Queen. Now, this play was the story of a man *who had been murdered in his garden by a near relation, who afterwards married the dead man's wife.*

You may imagine the feelings of the wicked King, as he sat on his throne, with the Queen beside him and all his Court around, and saw, acted on the stage, the very wickedness that he had himself done. And when, in the play, the wicked relation poured poison into the ear of the sleeping man, the wicked Claudius suddenly rose, and staggered from the room—the Queen and others following.

Then said Hamlet to his friends, "Now I am sure the ghost spoke true. For if Claudius had not done this murder, he could not have been so distressed to see it in a play."

Now the Queen sent for Hamlet, by the King's desire, to scold him for his conduct during the play, and for other matters; and Claudius wishing to know exactly what happened, told old Polonius to hide himself behind the curtains in the Queen's room. And as they talked, the Queen got frightened at Hamlet's rough, strange words, and cried for help, and Polonius, behind the curtain, cried out too. Hamlet, thinking it was the King who was hidden there, thrust with his sword at the hangings, and killed, not the King, but poor old Polonius.

So now Hamlet had offended his uncle and his mother, and by bad luck killed his true love's father.

"Oh, what a rash and bloody deed is this!" cried the Queen.

And Hamlet answered bitterly. "Almost as bad as to kill a king, and marry his brother." Then Hamlet told the Queen plainly all his thoughts, and how he knew of the murder, and begged her, at least, to have no more friendship or kindness for the base Claudius, who had killed the good King. And as they spoke the King's ghost again appeared

before Hamlet, but the Queen could not see it. So when the ghost was gone, they parted.

◆

Just at this time some actors came to the Court, and
Hamlet ordered them to perform a certain play.

When the Queen told Claudius what had passed, and how Polonius was dead, he said, "This shows plainly that Hamlet is mad, and since he has killed the chancellor, it is for his own safety that we must carry out our plan, and send him away to England."

So Hamlet was sent, under charge of two courtiers who served the King, and these bore letters to the English Court, requiring that Hamlet should be put to death. But Hamlet had the good sense to get at these letters, and put in others instead, with the names of the two courtiers who were so ready to betray him. Then, as the vessel went to England, Hamlet escaped on board a pirate ship, and the two wicked courtiers left him to his fate, and went on to meet theirs.

Hamlet hurried home, but in the meantime a dreadful thing had happened. Poor pretty Ophelia, having lost her lover and her father, lost her wits too, and went in sad madness about the Court, with straws, and weeds, and flowers in her hair, singing strange scraps of song, and talking poor, foolish, pretty talk with no heart of meaning to it. And one day, coming to a stream where willows grew, she tried to hang a flowery garland on a willow, and fell in the water with all her flowers, and so died.

And Hamlet had loved her, though his plan of seeming madness had made him hide it; and when he came back, he found the King and Queen, and the Court, weeping at the funeral of his dear love and lady.

Ophelia's brother, Laertes, had also just come to Court to ask justice for the death of his father, old Polonius; and now, wild with grief, he leaped into his sister's grave, to clasp her in his arms once more.

"I loved her more than forty thousand brothers," cried Hamlet, and leaped into the grave after him, and they fought till they were parted.

Afterwards Hamlet begged Laertes to forgive him.

"I could not bear," he said, "that any, even a brother, should seem to love her more than I."

But the wicked Claudius would not let them be friends. He told Laertes how Hamlet had killed old Polonius, and between them they made a plot to slay Hamlet by treachery.

Laertes challenged him to a fencing match, and all the Court were present. Hamlet had the blunt foil always used in fencing, but Laertes had prepared for himself a sword, sharp, and tipped with poison. And the wicked King had made ready a bowl of poisoned wine, which he meant to give poor Hamlet when he should grow warm with the sword play, and should call for a drink.

So Laertes and Hamlet fought, and Laertes, after some fencing, gave Hamlet a sharp sword thrust. Hamlet, angry at this treachery—for they had been fencing, not as men fight, but as they play—closed with Laertes in a struggle; both dropped their swords, and when they picked them up again, Hamlet, without noticing it, had exchanged his own blunt sword for Laertes's sharp and poisoned one. And with one thrust of it he pierced Laertes, who fell dead by his own treachery.

At this moment the Queen cried out, "The drink, the drink! Oh, my dear Hamlet! I am poisoned!"

She had drunk of the poisoned bowl the King had prepared for Hamlet, and the King saw the Queen, whom, wicked as he was, he really loved, fall dead by his means.

Then Ophelia being dead, and Polonius, and the Queen, and Laertes, besides the two courtiers who had been sent to England, Hamlet at last got him courage to do the ghost's bidding and avenge his father's murder—which, if he had found the heart to do long before, all these lives had been spared, and none suffered but the wicked King, who well deserved to die.

Hamlet, his heart at last being great enough to do the deed he ought, turned the poisoned sword on the false King.

"Then—venom—do thy work!" he cried, and the King died.

So Hamlet in the end kept the promise he had made his father. And all

So Hamlet in the end kept the promise he had made his father.
And all being now accomplished, he himself died.

being now accomplished, he himself died. And those who stood by saw him die, with prayers and tears for his friends, and his people who loved him with their whole hearts. Thus ends the tragic tale of Hamlet, Prince of Denmark.

The Tempest

$\mathcal{P}$rospero, the Duke of Milan, was a learned and studious man, who lived among his books, leaving the management of his dukedom to his brother Antonio, in whom indeed he had complete trust. But that trust was ill-rewarded, for Antonio wanted to wear the duke's crown himself, and, to gain his ends, would have killed his brother but for the love the people bore him. However, with the help of Prospero's great enemy, Alonso, King of Naples, he managed to get into his hands the dukedom with all its honor, power, and riches. For they took Prospero to sea, and when they were far away from land, forced him into a little boat with no tackle, mast, or sail. In their cruelty and hatred they put his little daughter, Miranda (not yet three years old), into the boat with him, and sailed away, leaving them to their fate.

But one among the courtiers with Antonio was true to his rightful master, Prospero. To save the duke from his enemies was impossible, but much could be done to remind him of a subject's love. So this worthy lord, whose name was Gonzalo, secretly placed in the boat some fresh water, provisions, and clothes, and what Prospero valued most of all, some of his precious books.

The boat was cast on an island, and Prospero and his little one landed in safety. Now this island was enchanted, and for years had lain under the spell of an evil witch, Sycorax, who had imprisoned in the trunks of trees all the good spirits she found there. She died shortly before Prospero was cast on those shores, but the spirits, of whom Ariel was the chief, still remained in their prisons.

Prospero was a great magician, for he had devoted himself almost entirely to the study of magic during the years in which he allowed his brother to manage the affairs of Milan. By his art he set free the imprisoned spirits, yet kept them obedient to his will, and they were more truly his subjects than his people in Milan had been. For he treated them kindly as long as they did his bidding, and he exercised his power over them wisely and well. One creature alone he found it necessary to treat with harshness: this was Caliban, the son of the wicked old witch, a hideous, deformed monster, horrible to look on, and vicious and brutal in all his habits.

When Miranda was grown up into a maiden, sweet and fair to see, it chanced that Antonio, and Alonso with Sebastian, his brother, and Ferdinand, his son, were at sea together with old Gonzalo, and their ship came near Prospero's island. Prospero, knowing they were there, raised by his art a great storm, so that even the sailors on board gave themselves up for lost; and first among them all Prince Ferdinand leaped into the sea, and his father thought in his grief he was drowned. But Ariel brought him safe ashore; and all the rest of the crew, although they were washed overboard, were landed unhurt in different parts of the island, and the good ship herself, which they all thought had been wrecked, lay at anchor in the harbor where Ariel had brought her. Such wonders could Prospero and his spirits perform.

While yet the tempest was raging, Prospero showed his daughter the brave ship laboring in the rough sea, and told her that it was filled with living human beings like themselves. She, in pity of their lives, prayed him who had raised this storm to quell it. Then her father bade her to have no fear, for he intended to save every one of them.

Then, for the first time, he told her the story of his life and hers, and that he had caused this storm to rise in order that his enemies, Antonio and Alonso, who were on board, might be delivered into his hands.

When he had made an end of his story he charmed her into sleep, for Ariel was at hand, and he had work for him to do. Ariel, who longed for his complete freedom, grumbled to be kept in drudgery, but on being threateningly reminded of all the sufferings he had undergone when Sycorax ruled in the land, and of the debt of gratitude he owed to the master who had made those sufferings to end, he ceased to complain, and promised faithfully to do whatever Prospero might command.

"Do so," said Prospero, "and in two days I will discharge thee."

Then he bade Ariel take the form

of a water nymph and sent him in search of the young prince. And Ariel, invisible to Ferdinand, hovered near him, singing the while:

◆

The boat was cast on an island, and Prospero and his little one landed in safety. Now this island was enchanted . . . under the spell of an evil witch.

Ariel, who longed for his complete freedom, grumbled to be kept in drudgery, but . . . promised faithfully to do whatever Prospero might command.

"Come unto these yellow sands,
And then take hands:
Court'sied when you have, and kiss'd,—
The wild waves whist,—
Foot it featly here and there;
And, sweet sprites, the burden bear."

And Ferdinand followed the magic singing, as the song changed to a solemn air, and the words brought grief to his heart, and tears to his eyes, for thus they ran:

"Full fathom five thy father lies;
Of his bones are coral made:
Those are pearls that were his eyes:
Nothing of him that doth fade,
But doth suffer a sea-change
Into something rich and strange.
Sea-nymphs hourly ring his knell.
Hark! now I hear them,—ding dong bell."

And so singing, Ariel led the spell-bound prince into the presence of Prospero and Miranda. Then, behold! all happened as Prospero desired. For Miranda, who had never, since she could first remember, seen any human being save her father, looked on the youthful prince with reverence in her eyes, and love in her secret heart.

"I might call him," she said, "a thing divine, for nothing natural I ever saw so noble!"

And Ferdinand, beholding her beauty with wonder and delight, exclaimed:

"Most sure, the goddess on whom these airs attend!"

Nor did he attempt to hide the passion which she inspired in him, for scarcely had they exchanged half a dozen sentences, before he vowed to make her his queen if she were willing. But Prospero, though secretly delighted, pretended wrath.

"You come here as a spy," he said to Ferdinand. "I will manacle your neck and feet together, and you shall feed on fresh water mussels, withered roots and husk, and have sea-water to drink. Follow."

"No," said Ferdinand, and drew his sword. But on the instant Prospero charmed him so that he stood there like a statue, still as stone; and Miranda in terror begged her father to have mercy on her lover. But he harshly refused her, and made Ferdinand follow him to his cell. There he set the prince to work, making him remove thousands of heavy logs of timber and pile them up; and Ferdinand patiently obeyed, and thought his toil all too well repaid by the sympathy of the sweet Miranda.

She in very pity would have helped him in his hard work, but he would not let her, yet he could not keep from her the secret of his love, and she, hearing it, rejoiced and promised to be his wife.

Then he bade Ariel take the form of a water nymph and sent him in search of the young prince. And Ariel, invisible to Ferdinand, hovered near him.

Then Prospero released him from his servitude, and glad at heart, he gave his consent to their marriage.

"Take her," he said, "she is thine own."

In the meantime, Antonio and Sebastian in another part of the island were plotting the murder of Alonso, the King of Naples, for Ferdinand being dead, as they thought, Sebastian would succeed to the throne on Alonso's death. And they would have carried out their wicked purpose while Alonso was asleep, except Ariel woke him in good time.

Many tricks did Ariel play on them. Once he set a banquet before them, and just as they were going to fall to, he appeared to them amid thunder and lightning in the form of a harpy, and immediately the banquet disappeared. Then Ariel upbraided them with their sins and vanished too.

Prospero by his enchantments drew them all to the grove near his cell, where they waited, trembling and afraid, and now at last bitterly repenting them of their sins.

Prospero determined to make one last use of his magic power, "and then," said he, "I'll break my staff and deeper than did ever plummet sound I'll drown my book."

So he made heavenly music to sound in the air, and appeared to them in his proper shape as the Duke of Milan. Because they repented, he forgave them and told them the story of his life since they had cruelly committed him and his baby daughter to the mercy of the wind and waves. Alonso, who seemed sorriest of them all for his past crimes, lamented the loss of his heir. But Prospero drew back a curtain and showed them Ferdinand and Miranda playing at chess. Great was Alonso's joy to greet his loved son again, and when he heard that the fair maid with whom Ferdinand was playing was Prospero's daughter, and that the young folks were engaged to be married, he said:

"Give me your hands, let grief and sorrow still embrace his heart that doth not wish you joy."

So all ended happily. The ship was safe in the harbor, and next day they all set sail for Naples, where Ferdinand and Miranda were to be married. Ariel gave them calm seas and auspicious gales; and many were the rejoicings at the wedding.

Then Prospero, after many years of absence, went back to his own dukedom, where he was welcomed with great joy by his faithful subjects. He practiced the arts of magic no more, but his life was happy, and not only because he had found his own again, but chiefly because, when his bitterest foes who had done him deadly wrong lay at his mercy, he took no vengeance on them, but nobly forgave them.

As for Ariel, Prospero made him free as air, so that he could wander where he would, and sing with a light heart his sweet song.

"Where the bee sucks, there suck I:
In a cowslip's bell I lie;
There I couch when owls do cry.
On the bat's back I do fly
After summer merrily:
Merrily, merrily shall I live now
Under the blossom that hangs on the bough."

King Lear was old and tired. He was weary of the business of his kingdom,
and wished only to end his days quietly near his three daughters.

King Lear

King Lear was old and tired. He was weary of the business of his kingdom, and wished only to end his days quietly near his three daughters, whom he loved dearly. Two of his daughters were married to the Dukes of Albany and Cornwall; and the Duke of Burgundy and the King of France were both staying at Lear's Court as suitors for the hand of Cordelia, his youngest daughter.

Lear called his three daughters together, and told them that he proposed to divide his kingdom between them. "But first," said he, "I should like to know how much you love me."

Goneril, who was really a very wicked woman, and did not love her father at all, said she loved him more than words could say; she loved him dearer than eyesight, space, or liberty, more than life, grace, health, beauty, and honor.

"If you love me as much as this," said the King, "I give you a third part of my kingdom. And how much does Regan love me?"

"I love you as much as my sister and more," professed Regan, "since I care for nothing but my father's love."

Lear was very much pleased with Regan's professions, and gave her another third part of his fair kingdom. Then he turned to his youngest daughter, Cordelia. "Now, our joy, though last not least," he said, "the best part of my kingdom have I kept for you. What can you say?"

"Nothing, my lord," answered Cordelia.

"Nothing?"

"Nothing," said Cordelia.

"Nothing can come of nothing. Speak again," said the King.

And Cordelia answered, "I love your Majesty according to my duty—no more, no less."

And this she said, because she knew her sisters' wicked hearts, and was disgusted with the way in which they professed unbounded and impossible love, when really they had not even a right sense of duty to their old father.

"I am your daughter," she went on, "and you have brought me up and loved me, and I return you those duties back as are right fit, obey you, love you, and most honor you."

Lear, who loved Cordelia best, had wished her to make more extravagant professions of love than her sisters; and what seemed to him her coldness so angered him that he bade her begone from his sight. "Go," he said, "be for ever a stranger to my heart and me."

The Earl of Kent, one of Lear's favorite courtiers and captains, tried to say a word for Cordelia's sake, but Lear would not listen. He divided the remaining part of his kingdom between Goneril and Regan, who had pleased him with their foolish flattery, and told them that he should only keep a hundred knights at arms for his following, and would live with his daughters by turns.

When the Duke of Burgundy knew that Cordelia would have no share of the kingdom, he gave up his courtship of her. But the King of France was wiser, and said to her, "Fairest Cordelia, thou art most rich, being poor—most choice, forsaken; and most loved, despised. Thee and thy virtues here I seize upon. Thy dowerless daughter, King, is Queen of us—of ours, and our fair France."

"Take her, take her," said the King; "for I have no such daughter, and will never see that face of hers again."

So Cordelia became Queen of France, and the Earl of Kent, for having ventured to take her part, was banished from the King's Court and from the kingdom. The King now went to stay with his daughter Goneril, and very soon began to find out how much fair words were worth. She had got everything from her father that he had to give, and she began to grudge even the hundred knights that he had reserved for himself. She frowned at him whenever she met him; she herself was harsh and undutiful to him, and her servants treated him with neglect, and either refused to obey his orders or pretended that they did not hear him.

Now the Earl of Kent, when he was banished, made as though he would go into another country, but instead he came back in the disguise of a serving-man and took service with the King, who never suspected him to be that Earl of Kent whom he himself had banished. The very same day that Lear engaged him as his servant, Goneril's steward insulted the King, and the Earl of Kent showed his respect for the King's Majesty by tripping up the steward into the gutter. The King had now two friends—the Earl of Kent, whom he only knew as his servant, and his Fool, who was faithful to him although he had given away his kingdom. Goneril was not contented with letting her father suffer insults at the hands of her servants. She told him plainly that his train of one hundred knights only served to fill her Court with riot and feasting; and so she begged him to dismiss them, and only keep a few old men about him such as himself.

"My train are men who know all parts of duty," said Lear. "Saddle my horses, call my train together. Goneril, I will not trouble you further—yet I have left another daughter."

And he cursed his daughter, Goneril, praying that she might never have a child, or that if she had, it might treat her as cruelly as she had treated him. And his horses being saddled, he set out with his followers

◆

The King had now two friends—the Earl of Kent . . . and his Fool, who
was faithful to him although he had given away his kingdom.

for the castle of Regan, his other daughter. Lear sent on his servant
Caius, who was really the Earl of Kent, with letters to his daughter to say
he was coming. But Caius fell in with a messenger of Goneril—in fact
that very steward whom he had tripped into the gutter—and beat him
soundly for the mischief-maker that he was; and Regan, when she heard
it, put Caius in the stocks, not respecting him as a messenger coming
from her father. And she who had formerly outdone her sister in professions of attachment to the King, now seemed to outdo her in undutiful
conduct, saying that fifty knights were too many to wait on him, that

five-and-twenty were enough, and Goneril (who had hurried there to prevent Regan from showing any kindness to the old King) said five and-twenty were too many, or even ten, or even five, since her servants could wait on him.

"What need one?" said Regan.

Then when Lear saw that what they really wanted was to drive him away from them, he cursed them both and left them. It was a wild and stormy night, yet those cruel daughters did not care what became of their father in the cold and the rain, but they shut the castle doors and went in out of the storm. All night he wandered about the countryside half mad with misery, and with no companion but the poor Fool. But presently his servant Caius, the good Earl of Kent, met him, and at last persuaded him to lie down in a wretched little hovel which stood upon the heath. At day-break the Earl of Kent removed his royal master to Dover, where his old friends were, and then hurried to the Court of France and told Cordelia what had happened.

Her husband gave her an army to go to the assistance of her father, and with it she landed at Dover. Here she found poor King Lear, now quite mad, wandering about the fields, singing aloud to himself and wearing a crown of nettles and weeds. They brought him back and fed him and clothed him, and the doctors gave him such medicines as they thought might bring him back to his right mind, and by-and-by he woke better, but still not quite himself. Then Cordelia came to him and kissed him, to make up, as she said, for the cruelty of her sisters. At first he hardly knew her.

"Pray do not mock me," he said. "I am a very foolish, fond old man, and to speak plainly, I fear I am not in my perfect mind. I think I should know you, though I do not know these garments, nor do I know where I lodged last night. Do not laugh at me, though, as I am a man, I think this lady must be my daughter, Cordelia."

"And so I am—I am," cried Cordelia. "Come with me."

◆

"Pray do not mock me," he said. "I am a very foolish, fond old man, and to speak plainly, I fear I am not in my perfect mind."

"You must bear with me," said Lear; "forget and forgive. I am old and foolish."

And now he knew at last which of his children it was that had loved him best, and who was worthy of his love; and from that time they were not parted.

Goneril and Regan joined their armies to fight Cordelia's army, and were successful: and Cordelia and her father were thrown into prison. Then Goneril's husband, the Duke of Albany, who was a good man, and had not known how wicked his wife was, heard the truth of the whole story; and when Goneril found that her husband knew her for the wicked woman she was, she killed herself, having a little time before given a deadly poison to her sister, Regan, out of a spirit of jealousy.

But they had arranged that Cordelia should be hanged in prison, and though the Duke of Albany sent messengers at once, it was too late. The old King came staggering into the tent of the Duke of Albany, carrying the body of his dear daughter Cordelia in his arms.

"Oh, she is gone forever," he said. "I know when one is dead, and when one lives. She's dead as earth."

They crowded around in horror.

"Oh, if she lives," said the King, "it is a chance that does redeem all sorrows that ever I have felt."

The Earl of Kent spoke a word to him, but Lear was too mad to listen.

"A plague upon you murderous traitors all! I might have saved her. Now she is gone forever. Cordelia, Cordelia, stay a little. Her voice was ever low, gentle, and soft—an excellent thing in woman. I killed the slave that was hanging thee."

" 'Tis true, my lords, he did," said one of the officers from the castle.

"Oh, thou wilt come no more," cried the poor old man. "Do you see this? Look on her—look, her lips. Look there, look there."

And with that he fell with her still in his arms, and died.

And this was the end of Lear and Cordelia.

While they were crossing a lonely heath, they saw three bearded women, sisters, hand in hand, withered in appearance and wild in their attire.

Macbeth

When a person is asked to tell the story of Macbeth, he can tell two stories. One is of a man called Macbeth who came to the throne of Scotland by a crime in the year of our Lord 1039, and reigned justly and well, on the whole, for fifteen years or more. This story is part of Scottish history. The other story issues from a place called Imagination; it is gloomy and wonderful, and you shall hear it.

A year or two before Edward the Confessor began to rule England, a battle was won in Scotland against a Norwegian King by two generals named Macbeth and Banquo. After the battle, the generals walked together toward Forres, in Elginshire, where Duncan, King of Scotland, was awaiting them.

While they were crossing a lonely heath, they saw three bearded women, sisters, hand in hand, withered in appearance and wild in their attire.

"Speak, who are you?" demanded Macbeth.

"Hail, Macbeth, chieftain of Glamis," said the first woman.

"Hail, Macbeth, chieftain of Cawdor," said the second woman.

"Hail, Macbeth, King that is to be," said the third woman.

Then Banquo asked, "What of me?" and the third woman replied, "Thou shalt be the father of kings."

"Tell me more," said Macbeth, "By my father's death I am chieftain of Glamis, but the chieftain of Cawdor lives, and the King lives, and his children live. Speak, I charge you!"

The women replied only by vanishing, as though suddenly mixed with air.

Banquo and Macbeth knew then that they had been addressed by witches, and were discussing their prophecies when two nobles approached. One of them thanked Macbeth, in the King's name, for his military services, and the other said, "He bade me call you chieftain of Cawdor."

Macbeth then learned that the man who had yesterday borne that title was to die for treason, and he could not help thinking, "The third witch called me, 'King that is to be.' "

"Banquo," he said, "you see that the witches spoke truth concerning me. Do you not believe, therefore, that your child and grandchild will be kings?"

Banquo frowned. Duncan had two sons, Malcolm and Donalbain, and he deemed it disloyal to hope that his son Fleance should rule Scotland. He told Macbeth that the witches might have intended to tempt them both into villainy by their prophecies concerning the throne. Macbeth, however, thought the prophecy that he should be King too pleasant to keep to himself, and he mentioned it to his wife in a letter.

Lady Macbeth was the grand-daughter of a King of Scotland who had died in defending his crown against the King who preceded Duncan, and by whose order her only brother was slain. To her, Duncan was a reminder of bitter wrongs. Her husband had royal blood in his veins, and when she read his letter, she was determined that he should be King.

When a messenger arrived to inform her that Duncan would pass a night in Macbeth's castle, she nerved herself for a very base action.

She told Macbeth almost as soon as she saw him that Duncan must spend a sunless morrow. She meant that Duncan must die, and that the dead are blind. "We will speak further," said Macbeth uneasily, and at night, with his memory full of Duncan's kind words, he would have preferred to spare his guest.

"Would you live a coward?" demanded Lady Macbeth, who seems to have thought that morality and cowardice were the same.

"I dare do all that may become a man," replied Macbeth; "who dare do more is none."

"Why did you write that letter to me?" she inquired fiercely, and with bitter words she egged him on to murder, and with cunning words she showed him how to do it.

After supper Duncan went to bed, and two grooms were placed on guard at his bedroom door. Lady Macbeth caused them to drink wine till they were stupefied. She then took their daggers and would have killed the King herself if his sleeping face had not looked like her father's.

Macbeth came later, and found the daggers lying by the grooms; and soon with red hands he appeared before his wife, saying, "Methought I heard a voice cry, 'Sleep no more! Macbeth destroys the sleeping!'"

"Wash your hands," said she. "Why did you not leave the daggers by the grooms? Take them back, and smear the grooms with blood."

"I dare not," said Macbeth.

His wife dared, and she returned to him with hands red as his own, but a heart less white, she proudly told him, for she scorned his fear.

The murderers heard a knocking, and Macbeth wished it was a knocking which could wake the dead. It was the knocking of Macduff, the chieftain of Fife, who had been told by Duncan to visit him early. Macbeth went to him, and showed him the door of the King's room.

Macduff entered, and came out again crying, "O horror! Horror! Horror!"

Macbeth appeared as horror-stricken as Macduff, and pretending that he could not bear to see life in Duncan's murderers, he killed the two grooms with their own daggers before they could proclaim their innocence.

These murders did not arouse suspicion, and Macbeth was crowned at Scone. One of Duncan's sons went to Ireland, the other to England. Macbeth was King. But he was discontented. The prophecy concerning Banquo oppressed his mind. If Fleance were to rule, a son of Macbeth would not rule. Macbeth determined, therefore, to murder both Banquo and his son. He hired two ruffians, who slew Banquo one night when he was on his way with Fleance to a banquet which Macbeth was giving for his nobles. Fleance escaped.

Meanwhile Macbeth and his queen received their guests very graciously, and he expressed a wish for them which has been uttered thousands of times since his day—"Now good digestion wait on appetite, and health on both."

"We pray your Majesty to sit with us," said Lennox, a Scotch noble; but before he could reply, the ghost of Banquo entered the banqueting hall and sat in Macbeth's place.

Not noticing the ghost, Macbeth observed that, if Banquo were present, he could say that he had collected under his roof the choicest chivalry of Scotland. Macduff, however, had curtly declined his invitation.

The King was again pressed to take a seat, and Lennox, to whom Banquo's ghost was invisible, showed him the chair where it sat.

But Macbeth, with his eyes of genius, saw the ghost. He saw it like a form of mist and blood, and he demanded passionately, "Which of you have done this?"

Still none saw the ghost but he, and to the ghost Macbeth said, "Thou canst not say I did it."

The ghost glided out, and Macbeth was impudent enough to raise a glass of wine "to the general joy of the whole table, and to our dear friend Banquo, whom we miss."

The toast was drunk as the ghost of Banquo entered for the second time.

"Begone!" cried Macbeth. "You are senseless, mindless! Hide in the earth, thou horrible shadow."

Again none saw the ghost but he.

"What is it your Majesty sees?" asked one of the nobles.

The Queen dared not permit an answer to be given to this question. She hurriedly begged her guests to leave a sick man who was likely to grow worse if he was obliged to talk.

Macbeth, however, was well enough the next day to converse with the witches whose prophecies had so depraved him.

He found them in a cavern on a thunderous day. They were revolving round a cauldron in which were boiling particles of many strange and horrible creatures, and they knew he was coming before he arrived.

"Answer me what I ask you," said the King.

"Would you rather hear it from us or our masters?" asked the first witch.

"Call them," replied Macbeth.

Thereupon the witches poured blood into the cauldron and grease into the flame that licked it, and a helmeted head appeared with the visor on, so that Macbeth could only see its eyes.

He was speaking to the head, when the first witch said gravely, "He knows thy thought," and a voice in the head said, "Macbeth, beware Macduff, the chieftain of Fife." The head then descended into the cauldron till it disappeared.

"One word more," pleaded Macbeth.

"He will not be commanded," said the first witch, and then a crowned child ascended from the cauldron bearing a tree in his hand. The child said—

"Macbeth shall be unconquerable till
The Wood of Birnam climbs Dunsinane Hill."

He found them in a cavern on a thunderous day. They were revolving
round a cauldron in which they were boiling particles of many strange
and horrible creatures, and they knew he was coming before he arrived.

"That will never be," said Macbeth; and he asked to be told if Banquo's descendants would ever rule Scotland.

The cauldron sank into the earth; music was heard, and a procession
of phantom kings filed past Macbeth; behind them was Banquo's
ghost. In each king Macbeth saw a likeness to Banquo, and he counted
eight kings.

Then he was suddenly left alone.

His next proceeding was to send murderers to Macduff's castle. They
did not find Macduff, and asked Lady Macduff where he was. She gave a

stinging answer, and her questioner called Macduff a traitor. "Thou liest!" shouted Macduff's little son, who was immediately stabbed, and with his last breath begged his mother to flee. The murderers did not leave the castle until all of its inhabitants were dead.

Macduff was in England listening, with Malcolm, to a doctor's tale of cures wrought by Edward the Confessor when his friend Ross came to tell him that his wife and children were no more. At first Ross dared not speak the truth, and turn Macduff's sympathy into sorrow and hatred. But when Malcolm said that England was sending an army into Scotland against Macbeth, Ross blurted out his news, and Macduff cried, "*All* dead, did you say? *All* my pretty ones and their mother? Did you say *all?*"

His sorry hope was in revenge, but if he could have looked into Macbeth's castle on Dunsinane Hill, he would have seen at work a force more solemn than revenge. Retribution was working, for Lady Macbeth was mad. She walked in her sleep amid ghastly dreams. She often washed her hands for a quarter of an hour at a time; but after all her washing, would still see a red spot of blood upon her skin. It was pitiful to hear her cry that all the perfumes of Arabia could not sweeten her little hand.

"Canst thou not minister to a mind diseased?" inquired Macbeth of the doctor, but the doctor replied that his patient must minister to her own mind. This reply gave Macbeth a scorn of medicine. "Throw physic to the dogs," he said; "I'll none of it."

One day he heard the sound of women crying. An officer approached him and said, "The Queen, your Majesty, is dead." "Out, brief candle," muttered Macbeth, meaning that life was like a candle, at the mercy of a puff of air. He did not weep; he was too familiar with death.

Presently a messenger told him that he saw Birnam Wood on the march. Macbeth called him a liar and a slave, and threatened to hang him if he had made a mistake. "If you are right you can hang me," he said.

From the turret windows of Dunsinane Castle, Birnam Wood did indeed appear to be marching. Every soldier of the English army held

◆

Macbeth still had his courage. He went to battle to conquer or die . . . and when Macduff came to him blazing for revenge, Macbeth said to him, "Go back; I have spilt too much of your blood already."

aloft a bough which he had cut from a tree in that wood, and like human trees they climbed Dunsinane Hill.

Macbeth still had his courage. He went to battle to conquer or die, and the first thing he did was to kill the English general's son in single combat. Macbeth then felt that no man could fight him and live, and when Macduff came to him blazing for revenge, Macbeth said to him, "Go back; I have spilt too much of your blood already."

"My voice is in my sword," replied Macduff, and hacked at him and bade him yield.

"I will not yield!" said Macbeth, but his last hour had struck. He fell.

Macbeth's men were in retreat when Macduff came before Malcolm holding a King's head by the hair.

"Hail, King!" he said; and the new King looked at the old.

So Malcolm reigned after Macbeth; but in years that came afterwards the descendants of Banquo were kings.

As You Like It

*T*here was once a wicked Duke named Frederick, who took the dukedom that should have belonged to his brother, and kept it for himself, sending his brother into exile. His brother went into the Forest of Arden, where he lived the life of a bold forester, as Robin Hood did in Sherwood Forest in England.

The banished Duke's daughter, Rosalind, remained with Celia, Frederick's daughter, and the two loved each other more than most sisters. One day there was a wrestling match at Court, and Rosalind and Celia went to see it. Charles, a celebrated wrestler, was there, who had killed many men in contests of this kind. The young man he was to wrestle with was so slender and youthful, that Rosalind and Celia thought he would surely be killed, as others had been; so they spoke to him, and asked him not to attempt so dangerous an adventure; but the only effect of their words was to make him wish to come off well in the encounter, so as to win praise from such sweet ladies.

Orlando, like Rosalind's father, was being kept out of his inheritance by his brother, and was so sad at his brother's unkindness that until he saw Rosalind, he did not care much whether he lived or died. But now the sight of the fair Rosalind gave him

◆

One day there was a wrestling match at Court, and
Rosalind and Celia went to see it.

strength and courage, so that he did marvelously, and at last Charles had
to be carried off the ground. Duke Frederick was pleased with his
courage, and asked his name.

"My name is Orlando, and I am the youngest son of Sir Rowland de
Boys," said the young man.

Now Sir Rowland de Boys, when he was alive, had been a good friend
to the banished Duke, so that Frederick heard with regret whose son
Orlando was, and would not befriend him, and went away in a very bad
temper. But Rosalind was delighted to hear that this handsome young
stranger was the son of her father's old friend, and as they were going
away, she turned back more than once to say another kind word to the
brave young man.

"Gentleman," she said, giving him a chain from her neck, "wear this for me. I could give more, but that my hand lacks means."

Then when she was going, Orlando could not speak, so much was he overcome by the magic of her beauty; but when she was gone, he said, "I wrestled with Charles, and overthrew him, and now I myself am conquered. Oh, heavenly Rosalind!"

Rosalind and Celia, when they were alone, began to talk about the handsome wrestler, and Rosalind confessed that she loved him at first sight.

"Come, come," said Celia, "wrestle with thy affections."

"Oh," answered Rosalind, "they take the part of a better wrestler than myself. Look, here comes the Duke."

"With his eyes full of anger," said Celia.

"You must leave the Court at once," he said to Rosalind.

"Why?" she asked.

"Never mind why," answered the Duke, "you are banished."

"Pronounce that sentence then on me, my lord," said Celia. "I cannot live out of her company."

"You are a foolish girl," answered her father. "You, Rosalind, if within ten days you are found within twenty miles of my Court, you die."

So Rosalind set out to seek her father, the banished Duke, in the Forest of Arden. Celia loved her too much to let her go alone, and as it was rather a dangerous journey, Rosalind, being the taller, dressed up as a young countryman, and her cousin as a country girl, and Rosalind said that she would be called Ganymede, and Celia, Aliena. They were very tired when at last they came to the Forest of Arden, and as they were sitting on the grass, almost dying with fatigue, a countryman passed that way, and Ganymede asked him if he could get them food. He did so, and told them that a shepherd's flocks and house were to be sold. They bought these with the money they had brought with them, and settled down as shepherd and shepherdess in the forest.

♦

Rosalind set out to seek her father, the banished Duke, in
the Forest of Arden. Celia loved her too much to let her go alone.

In the meantime, Orlando, because his brother Oliver wished to
take his life, also wandered into the forest, and there met with the rightful
Duke, and being kindly received, stayed with him. Now, Orlando could
think of nothing but Rosalind, and he went about the forest, carving
her name on trees, and writing love sonnets and hanging them on the
bushes, and there Rosalind and Celia found them. One day Orlando
met them, but he did not know Rosalind in her boy's clothes, though he
liked the pretty shepherd youth, because he fancied a likeness in him to
her he loved.

"There is a foolish lover," said Rosalind, "who haunts these woods
and hangs sonnets on the trees. If I could find him, I would soon cure
him of his folly."

Orlando confessed that he was the foolish lover, and Rosalind said,

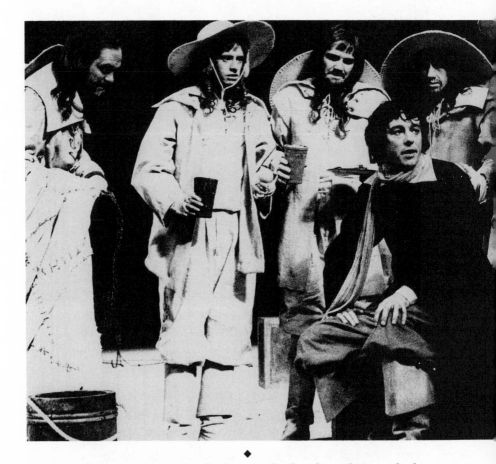

In the meantime, Orlando, because his brother Oliver wished to take his life, also wandered into the forest, and there met with the rightful Duke, and being kindly received, stayed with him.

"If you will come and see me every day, I will pretend to be Rosalind, and you shall come and court me, as you would if I were really your lady; and I will take her part, and be wayward and contrary, as is the way of women, till I make you ashamed of your folly in loving her."

And so every day he went to her house, and took a pleasure in saying

to her all the pretty things he would have said to Rosalind; and she had the fine and secret joy of knowing that all his love-words came to the right ears. Thus many days passed pleasantly away.

Rosalind met the Duke one day, and the Duke asked her what family "he came from." And Rosalind, forgetting that she was dressed as a peasant boy, answered that she came of as good parentage as the Duke did, which made him smile.

One morning, as Orlando was going to visit Ganymede, he saw a man asleep on the ground, and a large serpent had wound itself round his neck. Orlando came nearer, and the serpent glided away. Then he saw that there was a lioness crouching near, waiting for the man who was asleep, to wake: for they say that lions will not prey on anything that is dead or sleeping. Then Orlando looked at the man, and saw that it was his wicked brother, Oliver, who had tried to take his life. At first he thought to leave him to his fate, but the faith and honor of a gentleman withheld him from this wickedness. He fought with the lioness and killed her, and saved his brother's life.

While Orlando was fighting the lioness, Oliver woke to see his brother, whom he had treated so badly, saving him from a wild beast at the risk of his own life. This made him repent of his wickedness, and he begged Orlando's pardon with many tears, and from then on they were dear brothers. The lioness had wounded Orlando's arm so much, that he could not go on to see the shepherd, so he sent his brother to ask Ganymede ("whom I do call my Rosalind," he added) to come to him.

Oliver went and told the whole story to Ganymede and Aliena, and Aliena was so charmed with his manly way of confessing his faults, that she fell in love with him at once. But when Ganymede heard of the danger Orlando had been in, she fainted; and when she came to herself, said truly enough, "I should have been a woman by right." Oliver went back to his brother and told him all this, saying, "I love Aliena so well, that I will give up my estates to you and marry her, and live here as a shepherd."

"Let your wedding be tomorrow," said Orlando, "and I will ask the Duke and his friends. Go to the shepherdess—she is alone, for here comes her brother."

And sure enough Ganymede was coming through the wood towards them. When Orlando told Ganymede how his brother was to be married the next day, he added: "Oh, how bitter a thing it is to look into happiness through another man's eyes."

Then answered Rosalind, still in Ganymede's dress and speaking with his voice, "If you do love Rosalind so near the heart, then when your brother marries Aliena, shall you marry her. I will set her before your eyes, human as she is, and without any danger."

"Do you mean it?" cried Orlando.

"By my life I do," answered Rosalind. "Therefore, put on your best array and bid your friends to come, for if you will be married tomorrow, you shall—and to Rosalind, if you will."

Now the next day the Duke and his followers, and Orlando, and Oliver, and Aliena, were all gathered together for the wedding.

"Do you believe, Orlando," said the Duke, "that the boy can do all that he has promised?"

"I sometimes do believe and sometimes do not," said Orlando.

Then Ganymede came in and said to the Duke, "If I bring in your daughter Rosalind, will you give her to Orlando?"

"That I would," said the Duke, "if I had all kingdoms to give with her."

"And you say you will have her when I bring her?" she said to Orlando.

"That would I," he answered, "were I king of all kingdoms."

Then Rosalind and Celia went out, and Rosalind put on her pretty woman's clothes again, and after a while came back.

She turned to her father—"I give myself to you, for I am yours."

"If there be truth in sight," he said, "you are my daughter."

Then she said to Orlando, "I give myself to you, for I am yours."

"If there be truth in sight," he said, "you are my Rosalind."

"I will have no father if you be not he," she said to the Duke, and to Orlando, "I will have no husband if you be not he."

So Orlando and Rosalind were married, and Oliver and Celia, and they lived happily ever after, returning with the Duke to the dukedom. For Frederick had been shown by a holy hermit the wickedness of his ways, and so gave back the dukedom of his brother, and himself went into a monastery to pray for forgiveness.

The wedding was a merry one, in the mossy glades of the forest, where the green leaves danced in the sun, and the birds sang their sweetest wedding hymns for the new-married folk. A shepherd and shepherdess who had been friends with Rosalind, when she was herself disguised as a shepherd, were married on the same day, and all with such pretty feastings and merrymakings as could be nowhere within four walls, but only in the beautiful green-wood.

This is one of the songs which Orlando made about his Rosalind:

From the east to western Ind,
No jewel is like Rosalind.
Her worth, being mounted on the wind,
Through all the world bears Rosalind.
All the pictures, fairest lin'd
Are but black to Rosalind.
Let no face be kept in mind,
But the fair of Rosalind.

♦

Leontes was a violent-tempered man and rather silly, and he
took it into his stupid head that his wife, Hermione, liked
Polixenes better than she did him, her own husband.

The Winter's Tale

*L*eontes was the King of Sicily, and his dearest friend was Polixenes, King of Bohemia. They had been brought up together and only separated when they each had to go and rule over his own kingdom. After many years, when each was married and had a son, Polixenes came to stay with Leontes in Sicily.

Leontes was a violent-tempered man and rather silly, and he took it into his stupid head that his wife, Hermione, liked Polixenes better than she did him, her own husband. When once he had got this into his head, nothing could put it out; and he ordered one of his lords, Camillo, to put a poison in Polixenes's wine. Camillo tried to dissuade him from this wicked action, but finding he was not to be moved, pretended to consent. He then told Polixenes what was proposed against him, and they fled from the Court of Sicily that night, and returned to Bohemia where Camillo lived on as Polixenes's friend and counselor.

Leontes threw the Queen into prison; and her son, the heir to the throne, died of sorrow to see his mother so unjustly and cruelly treated.

While the Queen was in prison she had a little baby, and a friend of hers, named Paulina, had the baby dressed in its best, and took it to show the King, thinking that the sight of his helpless little daughter would soften his heart towards his dear Queen, who had never done him any wrong, and who loved him a great deal more than he deserved; but the King would not look at the baby, and ordered Paulina's husband to take it away in a ship, and leave it in the most desert and dreadful place he could find, which Paulina's husband, very much against his will, was obliged to do.

Then the poor Queen was brought up to be tried for treason in preferring Polixenes to her King; but really she had never thought of anyone except Leontes, her husband. Leontes had sent some messengers to ask the god, Apollo, whether he was not right in his cruel thoughts of the Queen. But he had not patience to wait till they came back, and so it happened that they arrived in the middle of the trial. The Oracle said:

"Hermione is innocent, Polixenes blameless, Camillo a true subject, Leontes a jealous tyrant, and the King shall live without an heir, if that which is lost be not found."

Then a man came and told them that the little prince was dead. The poor Queen, hearing this, fell down in a fit; and then the King saw how wicked and wrong he had been. He ordered Paulina and the ladies who were with the Queen to take her away, and try to restore her. But Paulina came back in a few moments, and told the King that Hermione was dead.

Now Leontes's eyes were at last open to his folly. His Queen was dead, and the little daughter who might have been a comfort to him he had sent away to be the prey of wolves and hawks. Life had nothing left for him now. He gave himself up to his grief, and passed many sad years in prayer and remorse.

The baby Princess was left on the sea-coast of Bohemia, the very kingdom where Polixenes reigned. Paulina's husband never went home to tell Leontes where he had left the baby; for as he was going back to the ship, he met a bear and was torn to pieces. So there was the end of him.

But the poor, deserted little baby was found by a shepherd. She was richly dressed, and had with her some jewels, and a paper was pinned to her cloak, saying that her name was Perdita, and that she came of noble parents.

The shepherd, being a kind-hearted man, took home the little baby to his wife, and they brought it up as their own child. She had no more teaching than a shepherd's child generally has, but she inherited from her royal mother many graces and charms, so that she was quite different from the other maidens in the village where she lived.

One day Prince Florizel, the son of the good King of Bohemia, was hunting near the shepherd's house and saw Perdita, now grown up to a charming woman. He made friends with the shepherd, not telling him that he was the Prince, but saying that his name was Doricles, and that he was a private gentleman; and then, being deeply in love with the pretty Perdita, he came almost daily to see her.

The King could not understand what it was that took his son nearly every day from home; so he set people to watch him, and then found out that the heir of the King of Bohemia was in love with Perdita, the pretty shepherd girl. Polixenes, wishing to see whether this was true, disguised himself, and went with the faithful Camillo, in disguise too, to the old shepherd's house. They arrived at the feast of sheep-shearing, and, though strangers, they were made very welcome. There was dancing going on, and a peddler was selling ribbons and laces and gloves, which the young men bought for their sweethearts.

Florizel and Perdita, however, were taking no part in this happy scene, but sat quietly together talking. The King noticed the charming manners and great beauty of Perdita, never guessing that she was the daughter of his old friend, Leontes. He said to Camillo:

"This is the prettiest low-born lass that ever ran on the green sward. Nothing she does or seems but smacks of something greater than herself—too noble for this place."

They arrived at the feast of sheep-shearing, and, though
strangers, they were made very welcome. There was dancing
going on, and a peddler was selling ribbons and laces and gloves.

And Camillo answered, "In truth she is the Queen of curds and cream."

But when Florizel, who did not recognize his father, called upon the strangers to witness his marriage to the pretty shepherdess, the King made himself known and forbade the marriage, adding, that if she ever saw Florizel again, he would kill her and her old father, the shepherd; and with that he left them. But Camillo remained behind, for he was charmed with Perdita, and wished to befriend her.

Camillo had long known how sorry Leontes was for that foolish madness of his, and he longed to go back to Sicily to see his old master. He now proposed that the young people should go there and claim the protection of Leontes. So they went, and the shepherd went with them, taking Perdita's jewels, her baby clothes, and the paper he had found pinned to her cloak.

Leontes received them with great kindness. He was very polite to Prince Florizel, but all his looks were for Perdita. He saw how much she was like the Queen Hermione, and said again and again:

"Such a sweet creature my daughter might have been, if I had not cruelly sent her from me."

When the old shepherd heard that the King had lost a baby daughter, who had been left upon the coast of Bohemia, he felt sure that Perdita, the child he had raised, must be the King's daughter, and when he told his tale and showed the jewels and the paper, the King perceived that Perdita was indeed his long-lost child. He welcomed her with joy, and rewarded the good shepherd.

Polixenes had hastened after his son to prevent his marriage with Perdita, but when he found that she was the daughter of his old friend, he was only too glad to give his consent.

Yet Leontes could not be happy. He remembered how his fair queen, who should have been at his side to share his joy in his daughter's happiness, was dead through his unkindness, and he could say nothing for a long time but:

"Oh, thy mother! thy mother!" and ask forgiveness of the King of Bohemia, and then kiss his daughter again, and then the Prince Florizel, and then thank the old shepherd for all his goodness.

Then Paulina, who had been high all these years in the King's favor, because of her kindness to the dead Queen Hermione, said, "I have a statue made in the likeness of the dead queen, a piece many years in doing, and performed by the rare Italian Master, Giulio Romano. I keep it in a private house apart, and there, ever since you lost your queen, I have gone twice or thrice a day. Will it please your Majesty to go and see the statue?"

So Leontes, and Polixenes, and Florizel, and Perdita, with Camillo and their attendants, went to Paulina's house, and there was a heavy purple curtain screening off an alcove; and Paulina, with her hand on the curtain, said:

"She was peerless when she was alive, and I do believe that her dead likeness excels whatever yet you have looked upon, or that the hand of

The King perceived that Perdita was indeed his long-lost child.
He welcomed her with joy, and rewarded the good shepherd.

man hath done. Therefore I keep it lonely, apart. But here it is. Behold,
and say 'tis well.

And with that she drew back the curtain and showed them the statue.
The King gazed and gazed on the beautiful statue of his dead wife, but
said nothing.

"I like your silence," said Paulina, "it the more shows off your wonder; but speak, is it not like her?"

"It is almost herself," said the King, "and yet, Paulina, Hermione
was not so much wrinkled, nothing like so old as this seems."

"Oh, not by much," said Polixenes.

"Ah," said Paulina, "that is the cleverness of the carver, who shows her to us as she would have been, had she lived till now."

And still Leontes looked at the statue and could not take his eyes away.

"If I had known," said Paulina, "that this poor image would so have stirred your grief, and love, I would not have shown it to you."

But he only answered, "Do not draw the curtain."

"No, you must not look any longer," said Paulina, "or you will think it moves."

"Let be, let be!" said the King. "Would you not think it breathed?"

"I will draw the curtain," said Paulina, "you will think it lives presently."

"Ah, sweet Paulina," said Leontes, "make me to think so twenty years together."

"If you can bear it," said Paulina, "I can make the statue move, make it come down and take you by the hand. Only you would think it was by wicked magic."

"Whatever you can make her do, I am content to look on," said the King. And then, all folks there admiring and beholding, the statue moved from its pedestal, and came down the steps and put its arms round the King's neck, and he held her face and kissed her many times, for this was no statue, but the real living Queen Hermione herself. She had lived, hidden by Paulina's kindness, all these years, and would not have discovered herself to her husband, though she knew he had repented, because she could not quite forgive him till she knew what had become of her little baby. Now that Perdita was found, she forgave her husband everything, and it was like a new and beautiful marriage to them, to be together once more. Florizel and Perdita were married, and lived long and happily. To Leontes his long years of suffering were well paid for, in the moment, when, after long grief and pain, he felt the arms of his true love round him once again.

Othello

*F*our hundred years ago there lived in Venice a soldier named Iago, who hated his general, Othello, for not making him a lieutenant. Instead of Iago, who was strongly recommended, Othello had chosen Michael Cassio, whose smooth tongue had helped him to win the heart of Desdemona. Iago had a friend called Roderigo, who supplied him with money and felt he could not be happy unless Desdemona was his wife.

Othello was a Moor, but of so dark a complexion that his enemies called him a Blackamoor. His life had been hard and exciting. He had been vanquished in battle and sold into slavery; and he had been a great traveler and seen men whose shoulders were higher than their heads. Brave as a lion, he had one great fault—jealousy. His love was a terrible selfishness. To love a woman meant with him to possess her as absolutely as he possessed something that did not live and think. The story of Othello is a story of jealousy.

One night Iago told Roderigo that Othello had carried off Desdemona without the knowledge of her father, Brabantio. He persuaded Roderigo to arouse Brabantio, and when that senator appeared Iago told him of Desdemona's elopement in the most

♦

Othello's love was a terrible selfishness. To love a woman meant with him to possess her as absolutely as he possessed something that did not live and think.

unpleasant way. Though he was Othello's officer, he termed him a thief and a Barbary horse.

Brabantio accused Othello before the Duke of Venice of using sorcery to fascinate his daughter, but Othello said that the only sorcery he used was his voice, which told Desdemona his adventures and hairbreadth escapes. Desdemona was led into the council-chamber, and she explained how she could love Othello despite his almost black face by saying, "I saw Othello's visage in his mind."

As Othello had married Desdemona, and she was glad to be his wife, there was no more to be said against him, especially as the Duke wished him to go to Cyprus to defend it against the Turks. Othello was quite ready to go, and Desdemona, who pleaded to go with him, was permitted to join him at Cyprus.

Othello's feelings on landing in this island were intensely joyful. "Oh, my sweet," he said to Desdemona, who arrived with Iago, his wife, and Roderigo before him, "I hardly know what I say to you. I am in love with my own happiness."

News coming presently that the Turkish fleet was out of action, he proclaimed a festival in Cyprus from five to eleven at night.

Cassio was on duty in the Castle where Othello ruled Cyprus, so Iago decided to make the lieutenant drink too much. He had some difficulty, as Cassio knew that wine soon went to his head, but servants brought wine into the room where Cassio was, and Iago sang a drinking song, and so Cassio lifted a glass too often to the health of the general.

When Cassio was inclined to be quarrelsome, Iago told Roderigo to say something unpleasant to him. Cassio hit Roderigo, who ran into the presence of Montano, the ex-governor. Montano civilly interceded for Roderigo, but received so rude an answer from Cassio that he said, "Come, come, you're drunk!" Cassio then wounded him, and Iago sent Roderigo out to scare the town with a cry of mutiny.

The uproar aroused Othello, who, on learning its cause, said, "Cassio, I love thee, but never more be officer of mine."

When Cassio and Iago were alone together, the disgraced man moaned about his reputation. Iago said reputation and humbug were the same thing. "O God," exclaimed Cassio, without heeding him, "that men should put an enemy in their mouths to steal away their brains!"

Iago advised him to beg Desdemona to ask Othello to pardon him. Cassio was pleased with the advice, and next morning made his request to Desdemona in the garden of the castle. She was kindness itself and said, "Be merry, Cassio, for I would rather die than forsake your cause."

Cassio at that moment saw Othello advancing with Iago, and retired hurriedly.

Iago said, "I don't like that."

"What did you say?" asked Othello, who felt that he had meant something unpleasant, but Iago pretended he had said nothing. "Was not that Cassio who went from my wife?" asked Othello, and Iago, who knew that it was Cassio and why it was Cassio, said, "I cannot think it was Cassio who stole away in that guilty manner."

Desdemona told Othello that it was grief and humility which made Cassio retreat at his approach. She reminded him how Cassio had taken his part when she was still carefree, and found fault with her Moorish lover. Othello was melted, and said, "I will deny thee nothing," but Desdemona told him that what she asked was as much for his good as dining.

Desdemona left the garden, and Iago asked if it was really true that Cassio had known Desdemona before her marriage.

"Yes," said Othello.

"Indeed," said Iago, as though something that had mystified him was now very clear.

"Is he not honest?" demanded Othello, and Iago repeated the adjective inquiringly, as though he were afraid to say "No."

"What do you mean?" insisted Othello.

To this Iago would only say the flat opposite of what he said to Cassio. He had told Cassio that reputation was humbug. To Othello he said, "Who steals my purse steals trash, but he who filches from me my good name ruins me."

At this Othello almost leapt into the air, and Iago was so confident of his jealousy that he ventured to warn him against it. Yes, it was no other than Iago who called jealousy "the green-eyed monster which doth mock the meat it feeds on."

Iago having given jealousy one blow, proceeded to feed it with the remark that Desdemona deceived her father when she eloped with Othello. "If she deceived him, why not you?" was his meaning.

Presently Desdemona re-entered to tell Othello that dinner was ready. She saw that he was ill at ease. He explained it by a pain in his forehead. Desdemona then produced a handkerchief, which Othello had

The unhappy Moor went mad with fury, and Iago asked the heavens to witness that he devoted his hand and heart and brain to Othello's service.

given her. A prophetess, two hundred years old, had made this handker-chief from the silk of sacred silkworms, dyed it in a liquid prepared from the hearts of maidens, and embroidered it with strawberries. Gentle Des-demona thought of it simply as a cool, soft thing for a throbbing brow; she knew of no spell upon it that would work destruction for her who lost it. "Let me tie it round your head," she said to Othello; "you will be well in an hour." But Othello angrily said it was too small, and let it fall. Des-demona and he then went indoors to dinner, and Emilia picked up the handkerchief, which Iago had often asked her to steal.

She was looking at it when Iago came in. After a few words about it he snatched it from her, and told her to leave him.

In the garden he was joined by Othello, who seemed hungry for the worst lies he could offer. He therefore told Othello that he had seen Cassio wipe his mouth with a handkerchief, which, because it was spotted with strawberries, he guessed to be the one that Othello had given his wife.

The unhappy Moor went mad with fury, and Iago asked the heavens to witness that he devoted his hand and heart and brain to Othello's ser-vice. "I accept your love," said Othello. "Within three days let me hear that Cassio is dead."

Iago's next step was to leave Desdemona's handkerchief in Cassio's room. Cassio saw it and knew it was not his, but he liked the strawberry pattern on it, and he gave it to his sweetheart Bianca and asked her to copy it for him.

Iago's next move was to induce Othello, who had been bullying Desdemona about the handkerchief, to play the eavesdropper to a con-versation between Cassio and himself. His intention was to talk about Cassio's sweetheart, and allow Othello to suppose that the lady spoken of was Desdemona.

"How are you, lieutenant?" asked Iago when Cassio appeared.

"The worse for being called what I am not," replied Cassio, gloomily.

"Keep on reminding Desdemona, and you'll soon be restored," said Iago, adding, in a tone too low for Othello to hear, "If Bianca could set the matter right, how quickly it would mend!"

"Alas! poor rogue," said Cassio, "I really think she loves me," and like the talkative fellow he was, Cassio was led on to boast of Bianca's fondness for him, while Othello imagined, with choked rage, that he spoke of Desdemona, and thought, "I see your nose, Cassio, but not the dog I shall throw it to."

Othello was still spying when Bianca entered, boiling over with the idea that Cassio, whom she considered her property, had asked her to copy the embroidery on the handkerchief of a new sweetheart. She tossed him the handkerchief with scornful words, and Cassio departed with her.

Othello had seen Bianca, who was in station lower, in beauty and speech inferior far, to Desdemona, and he began in spite of himself to praise his wife to the villain before him. He praised her skill with the needle, her voice that could "sing the savageness out of a bear," her wit, her sweetness, the fairness of her skin. Every time he praised her Iago said something that made him remember his anger and utter it foully, and yet he must needs praise her, and say, "The pity of it, Iago! O Iago, the pity of it, Iago!"

There was never in all of Iago's villainy one moment of wavering. If there had been he might have wavered then.

"Strangle her," he said; and "Good, good!" said his miserable dupe.

The pair were still talking murder when Desdemona appeared with a relative of Desdemona's father, called Lodovico, who bore a letter for Othello from the Duke of Venice. The letter recalled Othello from Cyprus and gave the governorship to Cassio.

Luckless Desdemona seized this unhappy moment to urge once more the suit of Cassio.

"Fire and brimstone!" shouted Othello.

"It may be the letter agitates him," explained Lodovico to Desdemona, and he told her what it contained.

"I am glad," said Desdemona. It was the first bitter speech that Othello's unkindness had wrung out of her.

"I am glad to see you lose your temper," said Othello.

"Why, sweet Othello?" she asked, sarcastically; and Othello slapped her face.

Now was the time for Desdemona to have saved her life by separation, but she knew not her peril—only that her love was wounded to the core. "I have not deserved this," she said, and the tears rolled slowly down her face.

Lodovico was shocked and disgusted. "My lord," he said, "this would not be believed in Venice. Make her amends," but, like a madman talking in his nightmare, Othello poured out his foul thought in ugly speech, and roared, "Out of my sight!"

"I will not stay to offend you," said his wife, but she lingered even in going, and only when he shouted "Avaunt!" did she leave her husband and his guests.

Othello then invited Lodovico to supper, adding, "You are welcome, sir, to Cyprus. Goats and monkeys!" Without waiting for a reply he left the company.

Distinguished visitors detest being obliged to look on at family quarrels, and dislike being called either goats or monkeys, and Lodovico asked Iago for an explanation.

True to himself, Iago, in a round-about way, said that Othello was worse than he seemed, and advised them to study his behavior and save him from the discomfort of answering any more questions.

He proceeded to tell Roderigo to murder Cassio. Roderigo was out of tune with his friend. He had given Iago quantities of jewels for Desdemona without effect; Desdemona had seen none of them, for Iago was a thief.

Then Desdemona wept, but with violent words, in spite of all her pleading, Othello pressed upon her throat and mortally hurt her.

Iago smoothed him with a lie, and when Cassio was leaving Bianca's house, Roderigo wounded him, and was wounded in return. Cassio shouted, and Lodovico and a friend came running up. Cassio pointed out Roderigo as his assailant, and Iago, hoping to rid himself of an inconvenient friend, called him "Villain!" and stabbed him, but not to death.

At the Castle, Desdemona was in a sad mood. She told Emilia that she must leave her; her husband wished it. "Dismiss me!" exclaimed Emilia. "It was his bidding," said Desdemona; "we must not displease him now."

She sang a song which a girl had sung whose lover had been base to her—a song of a maiden crying by that tree whose boughs droop as though it weeps, and she went to bed and slept.

She woke with her husband's wild eyes upon her. "Have you prayed tonight?" he asked; and he told this blameless and sweet woman to ask God's pardon for any sin she might have on her conscience. "I would not kill thy soul," he said.

He told her that Cassio had confessed, but she knew Cassio had nothing to confess that concerned her. She said that Cassio could not say anything that would damage her. Othello said his mouth was stopped.

Then Desdemona wept, but with violent words, in spite of all her pleading, Othello pressed upon her throat and mortally hurt her.

Then with heavy heart came Emilia, and sought entrance at the door, and Othello unlocked it, and a voice came from the bed saying, "A guiltless death I die."

"Who did it?" cried Emilia; and the voice said, "Nobody—I myself. Farewell!"

"'Twas I that killed her," said Othello.

He poured out his evidence by that sad bed to the people who came running in, Iago among them; but when he spoke of the handkerchief, Emilia told the truth.

And Othello knew. "Are there no stones in heaven but thunderbolts?" he exclaimed, and ran at Iago, who gave Emilia her death-blow and fled.

But they brought him back, and the death that came to him later on was a relief from torture.

They would have taken Othello back to Venice to try him there, but he escaped them on his sword. "A word or two before you go," he said to the Venetians in the chamber. "Speak of me as I was—no better, no worse. Say I cast away the pearl of pearls, and wept with these hard eyes; and say that when in Aleppo years ago I saw a Turk beating a Venetian, I took him by the throat and smote him thus."

With his own hand he stabbed himself to the heart; and before he died his lips touched the face of Desdemona with despairing love.

Afterword

Peter Hunt

When Edith Nesbit (1858–1924) began to write her *Shakespeare Stories* in 1897, she had been a moderately successful writer for 12 years, but she was just beginning a career that would change the face of children's literature. Her first poems had been published in 1876 in the magazine *Good Words,* and she later remembered dreaming "of the days when I should become a great poet like Shakespeare." She became, instead, one of the world's greatest children's writers; with *The Story of the Treasure Seekers* in 1899, she established what is generally agreed to be a new tone of voice for writing for children, one that was neither patronizing nor didactic. In the books that followed, she blended fantasy and domestic realism in a new way, and her influence on 20th-century children's books has been incalculable.

Nesbit was also a very distinctive character: her biographer, Julia Briggs, has described her as "a mass of contradictions." In many ways she was a radical thinker; she was a founder of the middle-class, socialist Fabian Society, whose members included H. G. Wells and George Bernard Shaw; she flouted Victorian conventions by cutting her hair short, smoking (in public!), and wearing "aesthetic" clothes; and she wrote socialist poetry (such as *Ballads and Lyrics of Socialism, 1883–1908* [1908]).

Her domestic arrangements were also somewhat eccentric: her husband, Hubert Bland, a successful journalist, had many affairs with other women, which Edith tolerated, even bringing up as her own two children he had fathered by their live-in "companion-help." Bland seems to have had a powerful personality, and Edith, surprisingly, accepted some of his more conservative ideas—for example, that women were naturally inferior to men.

But, like her contemporaries Frances Hodgson Burnett and Louisa May Alcott, she was a strong woman among weak men, and for many years she supported her husband and family with her pen. (A fictionalized self-portrait appears in her 1906 novel *The Railway Children*.) Consequently, much of her work was potboiling material, including novels for adults, poems, plays, and large numbers of periodical contributions, many of them now lost. Examples were *All Round the Year* (1888), *The Girls' Own Birthday Book* (1894), *Pussy Tales and Doggy Tales* (1895), and *Royal Children of English History* (1897). Her versions of Shakespeare's plays, although sometimes included by critics in this workaday category, nevertheless throw a fascinating light on a writer learning her craft.

The Children's Shakespeare was published in Philadelphia in 1900, and Nesbit later produced *Twenty Beautiful Stories from Shakespeare* (Chicago, 1907 [Hertel, Jenkins] and 1926 [D. E. Cunningham]), subtitled "a home study course, being a choice collection from the World's greatest classic writer." To the modern eye, this is a very curious edition, as the illustrations are of pretty children playing the parts of Othello, Lady Macbeth, and the rest. These pictures clearly suited the "beautiful child" fashion of the period, but they are sometimes in grotesque contrast to—and in the case of the "bearded" and "withered" witches of *Macbeth* in direct contradiction to—the sometimes somber stories. Her third foray, *Children's Stories from Shakespeare* (London, 1910 [Raphael Turck]; Philadelphia, 1912 [David McKay]), included an essay called

"When Shakespeare was a Boy," by the distinguished radical writer and thinker F. J. Furnivall, founder of the Early English Text Society and a close friend of Kenneth Grahame. This edition was later reprinted as *Shakespeare Stories for Children*.

Nesbit's first adaptations of Shakespeare were obviously part of a popular fashion, for several other attempts appeared at the end of the century; these included *Shakespeare's Stories Simply Told* by Mary Seamer [afterwards Seymour] (1880), Adelaide [A. C. G.] Sim's *Phoebe's Shakespeare* (1894), M. Surtees Townesend's *Stories from Shakespeare* (1899), and *The Children's Shakespeare* by Ada B. Stidolph (1902). There had been several other attempts, in prose and verse, earlier in the century, but all had been overshadowed by the version by Charles and Mary Lamb, first published in 1808. There are echoes in Nesbit's version that suggest that she knew the Lambs' work, even if she did not actually have a copy open in front of her as she wrote.

Here, for example, is Nesbit's version of the opening of *Macbeth*:

> After the battle, the generals walked together. . . . While they were crossing a lonely heath, they saw three bearded women, sisters, hand in hand, withered in appearance, and wild in their attire. . . . The women replied only by vanishing, as though suddenly mixed with air. Banquo and Macbeth knew then that they had been addressed by witches, and were discussing their prophecies when two nobles approached. . . .

and here, Charles Lamb's:

> The two Scottish generals, Macbeth and Banquo, returning victorious from this battle, their way lay over a blasted heath, where they were stopped by the strange appearance of three figures like women, except that they had beards, and their withered skin and wild attire made them look not like earthly creatures. . . . They then turned into air, and vanished: by which the generals knew them to be the weird sisters, or witches. While they stood pondering on the strangeness of this adventure, there arrived certain messengers from the king. . . .

Reading the various versions, one has a good deal of sympathy with the adapters: Charles Lamb, according to Mary, would sit writing, "groaning all the while and saying he can make nothing of it." Nesbit clearly found, as her predecessors had done, that paring the flesh of Shakespeare's inimitable verse and prose from the plays can leave you with an unmanageable excess of plot, and there are times in her paraphrases (which are generally no more than a quarter of the length of the Lambs' versions) where little else is visible. Nonetheless, there is evidence that her versions have helped many children—who perhaps already trusted her as a writer—to find their way around the often complex stories.

In some cases Nesbit simplifies—Audrey and Touchstone are mentioned as an afterthought in *As You Like It*—and in the process some elements that she might have found politically incorrect or unsuitable for children are trimmed out: Shylock's Jewishness is not mentioned, and Macduff overcomes Macbeth by force of sword, not by any accident of birth. On occasion, the changes amount to editorial judgments, as in the final scene of *Hamlet,* in which the hero's own wound is played down in favor of his decision: "Hamlet at last got him courage to do the ghost's bidding."

The Children's Shakespeare does, however, have flashes both of the writer Nesbit was to become and of her political views. In *Romeo and Juliet,* the Montagus and Capulets get a slightly socialist treatment:

> They were both rich, and I suppose they were as sensible, in most things, as other rich people. But in one thing they were extremely silly. There was an old quarrel between the two families, and instead of making it up like reasonable folks, they made a sort of pet out of their quarrel . . .

Nesbit solved the problem of simplifying the language for younger readers in various ways. Quite often she quotes Shakespeare's lines directly, as when she includes Viola's lines from *Twelfth Night:* "She never told her love . . ." Elsewhere, she mixes extracts from the plays with more straightforward modern language. Sometimes—perhaps from the simple need for haste—the mixture of the old and the new results in a slightly unfortunate bathos. For example, here is Shakespeare's version of an early scene in *As You Like It*:

> *Celia*: Come, come, wrestle with thy affections.
> *Rosalind*: O, they take the part of a better wrestler than myself . . . Look, here comes the duke.
> *Celia*: With his eyes full of anger
>   *Enter* Duke Frederick *with* Lords
> *Duke Frederick*: Mistress, dispatch you with your safest haste
>   And get you from our court.
> *Rosalind*:   Me, Uncle?
> *Duke Frederick*:   You, cousin:
>   Within these ten days if that thou be'st found
>   So near our public court as twenty miles,
>   Thou diest for it.
> *Rosalind*: I do beseech your grace
>   Let me the knowledge of my fault bear with me. . . .
> *Duke Frederick*: Let it suffice thee that I trust thee not. . . .
>   Thou art thy father's daughter; there's enough.

And Nesbit:

> "Come, come," said Celia, "wrestle with thy affections."
> "Oh," answered Rosalind, "they take the part of a better wrestler than myself. Look, here comes the Duke."
> "With his eyes full of anger," said Celia.
> "You must leave the court at once," he said to Rosalind.
> "Why?" she asked.
> "Never mind why," answered the Duke, "you are banished. . . . You, Rosalind, if within ten days you are found within twenty miles of my Court, you die."

There is also a certain amount of swinging between two different kinds of anachronism—casual and slangy speech, and self-consciously grandiose archaisms. Thus the Duke in *As You Like It* "went away in a very bad temper," and Leontes "was a violent-tempered man and rather silly"; in contrast, Hamlet "by bad hap killed his true love's father"—although at the end he "at last got him courage." Occasionally, the collision occurs in the same sentence, as when Lady Macbeth "with bitter words . . . egged him on to murder." The modern reader, then, has to make some allowances for the curious linguistic byways into which Nesbit has strayed—and to sympathize with her when the subsequent development of the language has left oddities stranded, as it were, on the linguistic beach: "Then Paulina, who had been high all these years in the King's favor. . . ."

But if these stories show Nesbit the apprentice in her workshop, casting around for a satisfactory way to address children, some of the difficulties—although it may border on blasphemy to say so—are inherent in the original texts. Stripped of the subtleties of language, some of the machinations of the characters in, for example, *The Winter's Tale* and *The Tempest* can seem somewhat perverse. Equally, other plays, such as *Twelfth Night* and *The Merchant of Venice*, emerge as having strong, logical plots.

Edith Nesbit's *Shakespeare Stories* may not be the best known of her writings, but they show her learning her trade with particularly intractable materials. The relationship between adult writers and child readers is a difficult one and poses unique technical challenges to writers. To take complex pieces of drama and to shorten, simplify, modernize, sanitize, and make them accessible, in prose, to an audience that did not exist when they were written—the child as constructed by the 19th century—is a formidable task for any writer. Nesbit's versions may occasionally be uneven, but as we have seen, it may well be that they achieved their aim of helping children toward the "real thing." As Nesbit observed in her version of *Romeo and Juliet*:

> And the tale of all they said, and the sweet music their voices made together, is all set down in a golden book, where you children may read it for yourselves some day.

Picture Credits

Page 2: Ted van Griethuysen as Prospero in a 1989–90 production of *The Tempest* at The Shakespeare Theatre in Washington, D.C. Photo by Joan Marcus.

Page 11: Scene from the Stratford Festival's 1968 production of *Romeo and Juliet*. Courtesy the Stratford Festival Archives, Stratford, Ontario, Canada.

Page 14: Marin Hinkle as Juliet and Jay Goede as Romeo in a 1994 production of *Romeo and Juliet* at The Shakespeare Theatre in Washington, D.C. Photo by Richard Anderson.

Page 18: Scene from the Stratford Festival's 1960 production of *Romeo and Juliet*. Courtesy the Stratford Festival Archives, Stratford, Ontario, Canada.

Page 23: Scene from the Stratford Festival's 1970 production of *The Merchant of Venice*. Courtesy the Stratford Festival Archives, Stratford, Ontario, Canada.

Pages 24-25: Scene from the Stratford Festival's 1955 production of *The Merchant of Venice*. Courtesy the Stratford Festival Archives, Stratford, Ontario, Canada.

Pages 26-27: Scene from the Stratford Festival's 1976 production of *The Merchant of Venice*. Courtesy the Stratford Festival Archives, Stratford, Ontario, Canada.

Page 30: Kelly McGillis as Viola and Philip Goodwin as Malvolio in a 1989 production of *Twelfth Night* at The Shakespeare Theatre in Washington, D.C. Photo by Joan Marcus.

Pages 32-33: Kelly McGillis as Viola and Kate Skinner as Olivia in a 1989 production of *Twelfth Night* at The Shakespeare Theatre in Washington, D.C. Photo by Joan Marcus.

Page 35: Scene from the Royal Shakespeare Company's 1969 production of *Twelfth Night*. Photo courtesy the Shakespeare Centre Library, Stratford-upon-Avon, England.

Page 40: Richard Easton (left) as the Ghost and Roger Rees as Hamlet in the Royal Shakespeare Company's 1984 production of *Hamlet*. Photo courtesy the Shakespeare Centre Library, Stratford-upon-Avon, England.

Pages 42-43: Scene from the Stratford Festival's 1957 production of *Hamlet*. Courtesy the Stratford Festival Archives, Stratford, Ontario, Canada.

Pages 46-47: Scene from the Stratford Festival's 1969 production of *Hamlet*. Courtesy the Stratford Festival Archives, Stratford, Ontario, Canada.

Pages 50-51: Scene from the Royal Shakespeare Company's 1982 production of *The Tempest*. Photo courtesy the Shakespeare Centre Library, Stratford-upon-Avon, England.

Page 52: Louis A. Lotorto as Ariel in a 1990 production of *The Tempest* at The Shakespeare Theatre in Washington, D.C. Photo by Joan Marcus.

Pages 54-55: Scene from the Stratford Festival's 1992 production of *The Tempest*. Courtesy the Stratford Festival Archives, Stratford, Ontario, Canada.

Page 58: Scene from the Stratford Festival's 1972 production of *King Lear*. Courtesy the Stratford Festival Archives, Stratford, Ontario, Canada.

Page 62: Emery Battis as Lear and Philip Goodwin as the Fool in a 1991 production of *King Lear* at The Shakespeare Theatre in Washington, D.C. Photo by Joan Marcus.

Page 64: Sabrina LeBeauf as Cordelia and Fritz Weaver as Lear in a 1991 production of *King Lear* at The Shakespeare Theatre in Washington, D.C. Photo by Joan Marcus.

Page 66: Scene from the Royal Shakespeare Company's 1976 production of *Macbeth*. Photo courtesy the Shakespeare Centre Library, Stratford-upon-Avon, England.

Page 72: Scene from a 1988 production of *Macbeth* at The Shakespeare Theatre in Washington, D.C. Photo by Joan Marcus.

Page 74: Philip Goodwin (left) as Macbeth and Edward Gero as Macduff in a 1988 production of *Macbeth* at The Shakespeare Theatre in Washington, D.C. Photo by Joan Marcus.

Page 77: Scene from the Royal Shakespeare Company's 1967 production of *As You Like It*. Photo courtesy the Shakespeare Centre Library, Stratford-upon-Avon, England.

Page 79: Scene from a 1992 production of *As You Like It* at The Shakespeare Theatre in Washington, D.C. Photo by Joan Marcus.

Pages 80-81: Scene from the Royal Shakespeare Company's 1977 production of *As You Like It*. Photo courtesy the Shakespeare Centre Library, Stratford-upon-Avon, England.

Page 84: Ian McKellen in the Royal Shakespeare Company's 1976 production of *The Winter's Tale*. Photo courtesy the Shakespeare Centre Library, Stratford-upon-Avon, England.

Pages 88-89: Scene from the Royal Shakespeare Company's 1969 production of *The Winter's Tale*. Photo courtesy the Shakespeare Centre Library, Stratford-upon-Avon, England. Photographer: Morris Newcombe.

Page 91: Scene from the Royal Shakespeare Company's 1969 production of *The Winter's Tale*. Photo courtesy the Shakespeare Centre Library, Stratford-upon-Avon, England. Photographer: Morris Newcombe.

Page 94: Scene from the Stratford Festival's 1987 production of *Othello*. Photo by Michael Cooper. Courtesy the Stratford Festival Archives, Stratford, Ontario, Canada.

Page 97: Andre Braugher (left) as Iago and Avery Brooks as Othello in a 1990–91 production of *Othello* at The Shakespeare Theatre in Washington, D.C. Photo by Joan Marcus.

Page 101: Avery Brooks as Othello and Jordan Baker as Desdemona in a 1990–91 production of *Othello* at The Shakespeare Theatre in Washington, D.C. Photo by Joan Marcus.

E. NESBIT (1858-1924) is the author of many influential stories and novels for children, including *The Wouldbegoods* (1901), *The Phoenix and the Carpet* (1904), *The Railway Children* (1906), and *The Enchanted Castle* (1907). Her respect for children helped lay the groundwork for the direction of children's literature in the 20th century.

IONA OPIE is a noted authority in the field of children's lore and literature. With her late husband, Peter, she has edited and written many books on children's literature and games, including *The Oxford Dictionary of Nursery Rhymes, The Oxford Book of Children's Verse, The Classic Fairy Tales,* and *The Singing Game.* Their collection of children's literature is now housed at the Bodleian Library of Oxford University. Mrs. Opie's most recent work, *My Very First Mother Goose,* is a collaboration with acclaimed illustrator Rosemary Wells.

PETER HUNT is Professor of English and Children's Literature in the School of English at the University of Wales in Cardiff. His most recent books are *Children's Literature: An Illustrated History* and the *International Companion Encyclopedia of Children's Literature.*

ROBERT G. O'MEALLY is Zora Neale Hurston Professor of American Literature at Columbia University and previously taught English and Afro-American studies at Wesleyan University and Barnard College. He is the author of *The Craft of Ralph Ellison* and *Lady Day: Many Faces of the Lady* and editor of *Tales of the Congaree* by E. C. Adams and *New Essays on "Invisible Man."* Professor O'Meally is coeditor of *History and Memory in African-American Culture* and *Critical Essays on Sterling A. Brown.*

THE IONA AND PETER OPIE LIBRARY
OF CHILDREN'S LITERATURE

The Opie Library brings to a new generation an exceptional selection of children's literature, ranging from facsimiles and new editions of classic works to lost or forgotten treasures—some never before published—by eminent authors and illustrators. The series honors Iona and Peter Opie, the distinguished scholars and collectors of children's literature, continuing their lifelong mission to seek out and preserve the very best books for children.

ROBERT G. O'MEALLY, GENERAL EDITOR